insight text guide

Anica Boulanger-Mashberg

In the Country of Men

Hisham Matar

First published in 2013, reprinted in 2014, 2015, 2016, 2018.

Insight Publications Pty Ltd
3/350 Charman Road
Cheltenham VIC 3192
Australia
Tel: +61 3 9523 0044
Fax: +61 3 9523 2044
Email: books@insightpublications.com.au

www.insightpublications.com.au

National Library of Australia Cataloguing-in-Publication entry:
Boulanger-Mashberg, Anica.
Hisham Matar's In the Country of Men / Anica Boulanger-Mashberg.
9781922150981 (pbk.)
Insight text guide.
Includes bibliographical references.
Matar, Hisham, 1970– . In the country of men.
Matar, Hisham, 1970—Criticism and interpretation.
823.92

Other ISBNs:
9781925175103 (digital)
9781925175431 (bundle: print + digital)

Cover design: The Modern Art Production Group

Printed in Australia

contents

CHARACTER MAP

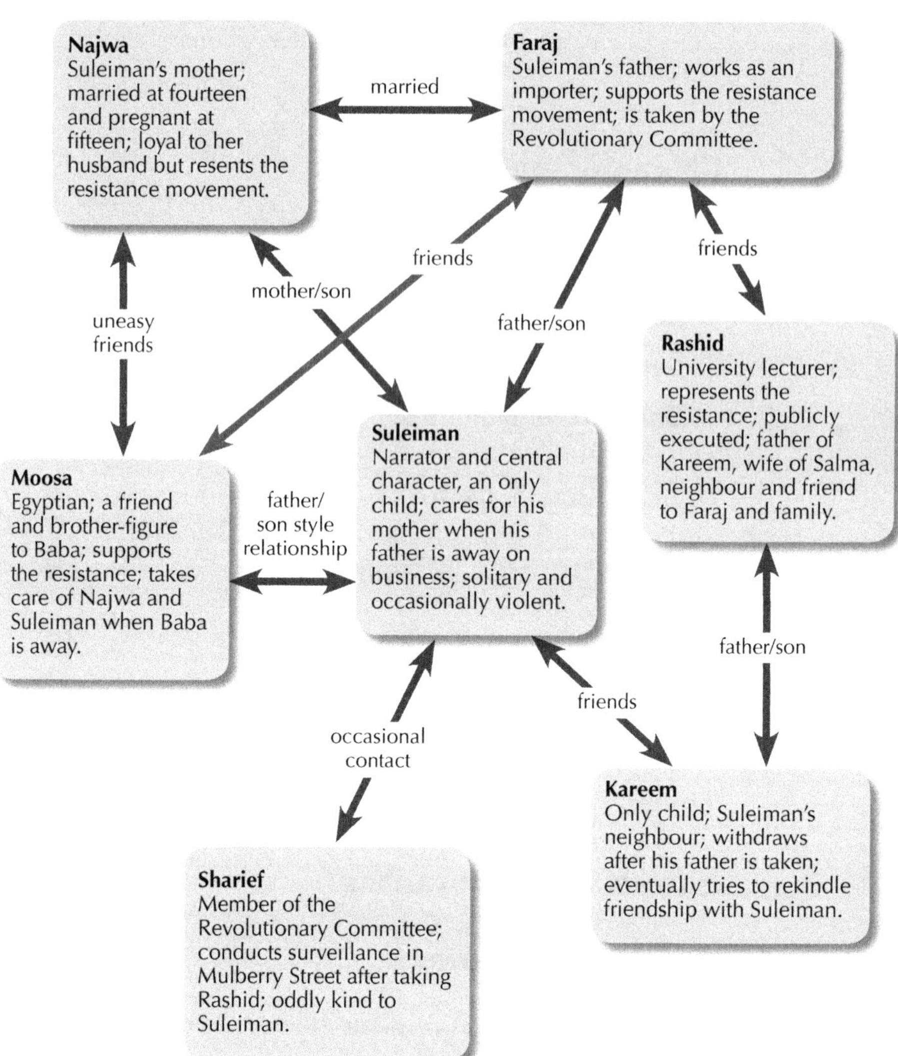

OVERVIEW

About the author

Hisham Matar was born in 1970 in New York City. His parents moved back to their home country of Libya soon after and lived in Tripoli until he was nine. His father, Jaballa, was considered a dissenter, opposed to the revolutionary politics and totalitarian rule of Muammar el-Qaddafi (better known in the West as Colonel Gaddafi). In order to protect his family, Jaballa Matar escaped with them to Cairo. Unfortunately Egypt could not continue to provide the safe haven for which he had hoped; in 1990 he was kidnapped.

Matar later discovered that his father had been taken back to Tripoli and kept in Abu Salim prison where detainees were subjected to incessant pro-revolutionary propaganda. Matar and his family received very occasional covert communications from his father or others who had contact with him, but after more than two decades they still had not seen him or received confirmation that he was alive (Matar 2010).

It is perhaps not surprising, then, that *In the Country of Men* (2006) describes a situation very similar to Matar's own: a young Libyan boy's father is captured and detained for his political views and activism. In the novel, though, the father returns (albeit damaged) to his family. Matar's second novel, *Anatomy of a Disappearance* (2011) also explores a father–son relationship and themes of loss, absence and political tyranny.

Matar himself has said that 'awards are inadequate for assessing good literature. They are very subjective ... But they remain a very effective way of highlighting new talent' (Musiitwa 2011). *In the Country of Men* was Matar's first novel, and its numerous awards gained him significant attention as a new talent. These awards include the inaugural Arab American Book Award and the Commonwealth Writers' Prize Best First Book Award (Europe and South Asia). The novel was shortlisted for a number of other prestigious awards including the Man Booker Prize and the Guardian First Book Award, and was included in the New York Times '100 Notable Books of 2007' list. It has been translated into many languages.

Synopsis

In the Country of Men portrays socially and politically turbulent Libya during the late 1970s through the eyes of nine-year-old Suleiman. The novel follows Suleiman throughout the last summer of his life in Libya, before he is sent by his parents to live in Cairo in the hope that he might escape some of the violence and danger they have faced in their lives.

The novel tells a personal and domestic story of familial loyalty, love, conflict and claustrophobia. This narrative of Suleiman's relationship with his parents is set against the broader political context of a country in the process of resisting the dictatorial reign of what was allegedly a democratic government.

Suleiman, an only child, is left alone with his mother whenever his father goes away on business. When she despairs and turns to drink, as she regularly does when her husband is away, Suleiman is responsible for her emotional and physical welfare and has an ambivalent relationship with this responsibility: he resents having to care for his mother when she is 'ill' yet harbours fantasies of rescuing her (even extending this desire to the past, when she was young, where he imagines he could have prevented her future suffering). During the summer of 1979, Suleiman's own challenges are put into a new perspective when first a friend and neighbour, and then his father, Baba, are detained by the Revolutionary Committee. The neighbour, Rashid, is executed as a traitor and although Baba is allowed to live, he is physically and psychologically scarred; he and his wife finally decide to send Suleiman to Cairo where he remains until the end of the novel, not even returning to Libya when Baba dies.

The novel is told principally from Suleiman's perspective as a child, with occasional shifts in the narrative perspective reminding us that it is an adult Suleiman who is narrating the story. Much of the novel is concerned with Suleiman's home life; intrusions from the rest of the world most often occur in the form of phone calls, visitors, televised interrogations or radio reports. Until Suleiman moves to Cairo, the majority of the scenes are set within the family house or garden, with only isolated excursions to the beach, town or schoolyard. Suleiman's interactions with characters other than his mother and father are limited, and his own thoughts and observations of the world are central to the novel.

Character summaries

Suleiman

Nine-year-old Suleiman is the central character. He tells the story from later in his life – in the final chapter he is twenty-four. An only child, he has close but ambivalent relationships with both of his parents, and looks up to other adults including Moosa and Ustath Rashid. (Also known as Slooma, Suleiman Faraj el-Dewani.)

Najwa (Mama)

Suleiman's mother, Najwa, was married to Faraj at fourteen and had Suleiman at fifteen. Her brothers and father arranged the marriage and she still resents it, although she cares for Faraj and is loyal to him. Her affection grows when he comes home after being tortured. She often turns to alcohol when Faraj is away on business, requiring Suleiman to care for her. (Also referred to as Mama, Naoma, Um Suleiman.)

Faraj (Baba)

Suleiman's father is an importer who often travels for work. He is older than his wife. He is considered a traitor by Qaddafi's regime because of his association with the underground resistance group plotting against it. (Also referred to as Baba, Faraj el-Dewani, Faraj Bu Suleiman el-Dewani, Bu Suleiman.)

Moosa

An old friend of Baba's, Moosa is a second father-figure for Suleiman, often visiting Suleiman and Najwa when Baba is away. It is Moosa who brings home the wounded Baba when he is finally released by the Revolutionary Committee. Moosa is the son of Judge Yaseen. Although originally from Egypt, Moosa considers himself Libyan and is loyal to the resistance movement. When he and his father are deported back to Egypt, they provide a home for Suleiman with them. (Moosa: Arabic version of the biblical Moses.)

Kareem

The son of Rashid and Salma, Kareem is Suleiman's next-door neighbour and best friend. Kareem is three years older than Suleiman, and he too is an only child. Suleiman thinks of him as a blood brother until Rashid's disappearance, when Suleiman becomes uneasy with his company. Many years later Kareem contacts Suleiman and makes an effort to re-open communication between them but Suleiman is unable to rekindle the friendship. Kareem eventually becomes engaged to Siham.

Ustath Rashid

Rashid, Kareem's father and Salma's husband, is professor of Art History at the el-Fateh University. Though he is absent for most of the novel, his story is central to it: he is seized by the Revolutionary Committee as a traitor, is interrogated and later is publicly executed. Rashid is a good friend of Baba's.

Salma

Rashid's wife and Kareem's mother, Salma is a close friend of Najwa until Rashid is taken, after which Najwa becomes frightened and cautious, avoiding contact with her neighbour. Salma has a brother in Benghazi (east of Tripoli) to whom she and Kareem travel after Rashid's death. (Also referred to as Auntie Salma.)

Nasser

Faraj's office clerk, Nasser is associated with the resistance movement. Faraj sees him as a younger brother and Suleiman reluctantly looks up to him.

Bahloul

Bahloul, the local beggar, is known to the community. Being mentally disturbed, he often rants, but sometimes the things he says appear to make sense and he is portrayed almost as a prophetic figure. Suleiman is physically cruel to him on several occasions, and attempts to drown him.

Sharief

Sharief is a member of the Revolutionary Committee who becomes familiar to Suleiman as the novel progresses. He is one of the men who take Rashid away; he is with the group who search the house for Baba; and he conducts regular surveillance in Suleiman's street. He tries to convince Suleiman that he is a friend of Baba's, in the hope of obtaining information.

Ustath Jafer and Um Masoud

Jafer is a member of the Mokhabarat: Qaddafi's intelligence agency. He and his wife, Um Masoud, are a threatening presence in Suleiman's street where several families don't support Qaddafi. When Mama eventually goes to them for help, they are instrumental in organising Baba's release. Ustath Jafer is 'rough and unrestrained' in his dealings with his wife (p.161). Their children, Masoud and Ali, are friends with Kareem, Suleiman and the other boys in the street. (Ustath Jafer is also called Bu Masoud.)

Minor characters

Adnan, a neighbourhood child. He suffers from an illness (an unnamed form of haemophilia) that affords him a certain importance among the other children. Suleiman accidentally injures him, alienating himself from the group.

Judge Yaseen, Moosa's father and eventually Suleiman's guardian; an important judge appointed by the overthrown King Idris.

Khaled, a poet and Najwa's brother; primarily responsible for his sister's arranged marriage after denouncing her to their family for socialising in public with a boy. (Also known as Uncle Khaled.)

Majdi, the baker and Najwa's supplier of illegal (and religiously prohibited) grappa (alcohol).

Masoud, Ali, Osama, other neighbourhood children.

Muammar el-Qaddafi, often called 'the Guide': the leader of the country after staging a coup in 1969 (the 'September Revolution') to overthrow King Idris. Qaddafi is not personally involved in the narrative but is a constant presence and an influence on the characters' lives.

Sheik Mustafa, Suleiman's Quran teacher, imam of the local mosque, blind.

Siham, Nasser's younger sister and eventually Kareem's fiancée (although Suleiman had loved her the first and only time they met).

BACKGROUND & CONTEXT

Libya

Libya, a country on the central north coast of Africa, is bordered by the Mediterranean Sea and six African countries, including Egypt to the east. Arabic is the country's official language and Tripoli, where Suleiman's family lives, is its capital and largest city.

The country's political history is complex; this guide provides only a basic overview of the historical and political background as it relates to the novel. For more detailed histories, refer to specific sources including those listed at the end of this guide.

In Chapter 3, Suleiman goes with Rashid's university students to Lepcis, where the remains of Libya's early history can be seen. The students and Suleiman are all familiar with this history, and when they visit the ruins they refer to the early Greek, Lebanese and Roman occupations and settlements. Matar doesn't expect us to gain a detailed historical understanding of the country; what is important is the students' familiarity with and connection to their history.

The area that would eventually become Libya was under the rule of the Ottoman (Turkish) Empire from the 1500s until Italian colonisation in the early 1900s. There are hints of the remaining Italian culture in the novel, including the Italian Coffee House where Najwa fatefully socialises with a boy when she is young. After the Italian occupation and a brief period of European administration following the Second World War, the country became independent in the 1950s, with its constitution ratified under its first and only king, King Idris, who ruled until he was overthrown by Qaddafi in 1969. This event, the 'September Revolution', is referenced in the novel. Qaddafi's Libya is the only one Suleiman has ever known.

Those who supported and implemented Qaddafi's rule were known as the Mokhabarat (the military intelligence agency). Not long before the events of the novel take place, Qaddafi had established Revolutionary Committees, whose purpose was to perpetuate the revolution and help enforce the regime's rule. Those who resisted, like Baba, Moosa and Rashid, were called traitors. The resistance was largely underground – it would not be until nearly forty years after the Revolution that civil war broke out and Qaddafi was finally removed from power. Under Qaddafi, Libya was ostensibly a democracy, but did not function as such. It is this totalitarian rule that has been in place for ten years when the novel opens, and which Baba and his friends and colleagues resist.

Religion

Islam was introduced to Libya in the early 1800s and remains the official religion of the country. *In the Country of Men* regularly alludes to the influence of religion on the lives of Libyans, including Suleiman and his family. The daily call to prayer can be heard from his house, and the spires of the local mosque are always visible. Suleiman's parents and friends often quote the Quran, or praise the Prophet.

A small story in a big context

Although the historical, political, religious and cultural contexts for the novel are detailed and complex, much of the narrative is domestic and Matar's text is generous, usually offering us the necessary cultural context to navigate the situation. The domestic storyline is one of father–son and mother–son relationships. The text is also concerned with the nature of freedom and betrayal, but while these issues are explored in the specific context of Libya in the 1970s, Matar does not require us to have a detailed understanding of the dynamics of the country. He conveys, through Suleiman, the impacts of such a society on a young boy who – like the reader – may not understand the intricacies of the country's politics.

The novel finds ways to impart small, important details to us without becoming didactic or self-conscious. For example, in the first chapter Suleiman is trying to avoid speaking with his mother. Conveniently, there is a prayer being read on the car radio: conveniently because, as Suleiman observes, 'everyone knows, one must refrain from speaking and listen humbly to the Quran when it is read' (p.2). This tells us that Suleiman and his family are devout Muslims. It also subtly offers us information we may not know about the traditions of the culture. Suleiman similarly conveys many other cultural norms, traditions and expectations – such as how they must invite Majdi the baker in when he delivers Mama's 'medicine', because 'it's impolite to just take what he had delivered from the door and leave it at that' (p.122).

GENRE, STRUCTURE & LANGUAGE

Genre

In the Country of Men is a realistic narrative novel, told in the first person in a style and structure similar to those of a nonfiction memoir. It documents one person's experience of a period of life in a very specific socio-cultural, geographical and temporal location. It is not quite an **autobiographical novel**; although many details resemble those in Matar's own life, one primary element of the story is the relationship between Suleiman and his mother, which has not been drawn from Matar's life.

There are numerous other differences, too; for example, Matar is not an only child. But the similarities are significant enough for it to be described as a **semi-autobiographical novel**: a novel that harnesses identifiable details from an author's life, but presents them within a new, fictional context. For example, Matar's father shares with Baba political commitment, and arrest and detention as a dissident. However, the events that follow differ significantly. Matar's father was kidnapped in Egypt, where he had taken his family for safety, and held for many years. In 2012, more than two decades after his disappearance, Matar's family still did not know where he was, or even if he was alive. In contrast, Baba is returned to his family and Suleiman is sent to Egypt on his own.

Literature and films often proudly proclaim their origins in 'real life'. Audiences seem to appreciate some grain of truth at the centre of their escapism. Why is this important to us? How does it change our reading of the text? Why does Matar choose to tell a fictional story rather than a 'true' story? And how do we know the novel is a novel – a work of *fiction* – and not an autobiography?

There is little technical difference between autobiographical writing and contemporary fiction. There are few 'rules' defining either genre, and the genres tend to be distinguished more by tone than either content or style. Yet, an autobiography could be written in a flowery, 'creative', even experimental style, while a novel might be detailed, concrete, conservatively structured and realistic. So the differences can be subtle.

Suleiman's story and Matar's story certainly share many features, though Hisham says that his life and Suleiman's life are 'very different' (Gilbert 2011). Both Matar and Suleiman lived through the Libya of 1979 as nine-year-olds. Matar, like Suleiman, grew up in Tripoli and Cairo, and he remains, in adult life, a part of the Libyan diaspora (people of a particular nationality and culture who live away from their homeland). Like Suleiman, Matar is an expatriate who tells a story of his home country with a mixture of nostalgia and judgement. He has a desire to show us a Libya that is cruel and frightening, yet is also a place he considers 'home'.

However, the novel never purports to tell us Matar's own story. In fact, he has said that he had 'no interest in writing an autobiographical account' of his childhood, preferring the unpredictability and surprises of imagination and fiction (Matar no date). Instead, *In the Country of Men* tells a story we can generalise: we realise that Suleiman's struggles and experiences resemble those of many children facing the transition from childhood to adulthood, whether in Libya or elsewhere.

The autobiographical novel can cause challenges in interpretation when the lines between fiction and nonfiction are blurred. For example, Australian writer Helen Garner's novel *The Spare Room* (2008) was so closely based on events from her own life that the central character even shared Garner's given name. The sometimes uncertain critical reception of the novel demonstrated the discomfort this can cause for audiences; when readers do not know whether the work is 'fact' or 'fiction', interpretation can be more difficult. Although *In the Country of Men* does not suffer from such blurring, the potential challenge for audiences is a reminder of the way our knowledge of genre influences our readings.

Q Can you identify literary techniques used in *In the Country of Men* that would not be appropriate in autobiography and therefore help us identify genre? What other clues to genre can you identify?

Q What reasons can you think of for Matar's choice of genre?

Structure

Despite the framework formed by the retrospective perspective of the adult Suleiman, with only two exceptions Matar's novel follows a naturalistic chronology. These exceptions to the chronological ordering of events within the timeframe of 1979 occur in the first two and final two chapters:

- The first two chapters are set approximately a week into the story, after Rashid is taken.
- The third chapter then takes the reader back to the beginning of the story.
- The following chapters proceed in chronological order through the summer.
- The final two chapters span the fifteen years Suleiman spends in Egypt following the end of the summer of 1979 until the day he sees his mother again.

In the Country of Men is comprised of short chapters that are often divided into smaller segments. Although the overall narrative is coherent, these short segments make each chapter feel episodic. This suits the childlike voice, suggesting that someone Suleiman's age has a limited attention span and thus processes events with a strong focus on the immediate present.

Language

Matar's style in *In the Country of Men* is often concrete and direct – as is appropriate for the voice of a nine-year-old child. Suleiman frequently relates events in simple, descriptive terms. For example, when he watches his father from the town square in the first chapter, Suleiman observes that Baba is 'standing on the edge of the pavement in a street opposite the square, looking both ways for traffic, arching forward as if he was about to fall' (p.5). The description is detailed and literal, focused on physical detail and with a sense of immediacy. This develops the childish voice, with its emphasis on the physical environment and concrete facts that the narrator can readily understand.

However, the novel embraces poetic expression too, and Suleiman sometimes slips into rich imagery. For example, as he continues to watch his father, he observes the sunglasses Baba wears: 'Two dark lenses curved like the humpbacks of turtles over his eyes' (p.5). The evocative simile used to describe the glasses demonstrates his ability to relate to the world in symbolic imagery as well as concrete description. Remember that the nine-year-old voice of Suleiman here is mediated by the intervening years, so the more sophisticated imagery is likely to reflect the adult-Suleiman's thought processes rather than those of his younger self.

Voice and the unreliable narrator

Classical scholarship identifies three kinds of narrator, with the second being one who 'assumes the voice of another person or persons' (Cuddon 1988, p.535). Although *In the Country of Men* contains multiple voices, they belong only to a single person. The first narrator we meet is the adult Suleiman of the present. He quickly introduces his nine-year-old self, who becomes the primary narrator for the novel. Although the narrator's knowledge is that of the adult Suleiman (which we see when the adult voice emerges occasionally, such as on pp.157–8), the 'voice' is usually that of a child. This means that his vocabulary, thought processes and comprehension reflect his age. A good example is his insistence on describing his mother's alcohol-induced state as 'illness' even once we become aware of the truth.

To an extent, the young Suleiman is also an example of what is known as an 'unreliable narrator'. This refers to a narrator whose knowledge, understanding or opinions differ somehow from that of the author, compromising the integrity of the narrator in some way and creating a kind of fissure or gap in which the reader may interpret the subtext. Here, the difference lies in Suleiman's inability to process and fully understand the events occurring during the summer. We are aware that his perception and comprehension are limited, but the 'adult' Suleiman rarely steps in to correct his younger self. Again, the way young Suleiman describes his mother's drinking is a key example. We know that his perception is flawed, yet he continues to narrate from this perspective.

Vocabulary

Although *In the Country of Men* is written in English, Matar uses Arabic words throughout, reminding us of the setting. (Definitions of some of these words appear in the Glossary at the end of this text guide; others are clear from their context and do not require definition.)

Note also that transliteration (taking words from one alphabet and language into the alphabet of another language) from Arabic to English is notoriously difficult and is not standardised. Therefore, you may find familiar names and words (such as Qaddafi or Quran) spelled quite differently from how you have seen them in other sources, such as contemporary Australian newspapers. Make sure, when writing about the novel, that you use the spellings Matar has chosen.

Arabic names in *In the Country of Men*

As you read the novel you will find that there are a number of variations on names for each character. This can be confusing at first, as the Arabic constructions of names are complex and differ significantly from English structures. As a basic guide to the Libyan names in the novel, full formal names include a personal name (similar to an English first name) and additional names which describe relationships to family: usually fathers and sometimes children. For example, Baba's full name can be explained as follows:

- Faraj = personal name
- Bu Suleiman = father of Suleiman
- el-Dewani = an additional descriptor – this can refer to a number of things including place of origin, family heritage or occupation.

Many familiar English surnames have a similar etymology; for example, 'Richardson' once literally meant 'son of Richard', and names such as 'Cooper' refer to occupation: coopers make or repair barrels. The meaning of 'Dewani' is not discussed in the novel.

Matar often uses nicknames for characters, which adds even more variation to names. Alternate forms of characters' names are included in the section 'Character summaries' on pp.3–6 of this guide.

'Suleiman' is the Arabic equivalent of the biblical 'Solomon'; Suleiman is also known by his nickname, 'Slooma'; and his mother often uses the generic nickname 'habibi', an Arabic term of affection for males. Suleiman refers to his parents by the affectionate, familiar forms of parental address, 'Mama' and 'Baba'. ('Baba' is not only an Arabic term for 'father' but is also used as a more general term of endearment. It is also found in many other languages as a word for father.) His parents refer to each other sometimes in this way too, and at other times by their names, Najwa – or the nickname 'Naoma' to her family and those close to her – and Faraj. Baba also calls Mama 'Um Suleiman' (p.51).

The forms 'Ustath [personal name]' and 'Um [personal name]' (as in 'Ustath Rashid') are similar to the English 'Mr' and 'Mrs' – terms of formal address. Note, however, that 'Um' precedes the name of the woman's child (usually the oldest son) rather than a family name, so 'Um' defines the woman as a mother, where 'Mrs' defines her as a wife. 'Ustath' is also the word for a professor or teacher, so its generic use as a formal address is an indication of the respect traditionally afforded to males.

Q How does Matar incorporate Arabic words into his English text? How do we understand their meaning?

Q How do we know the difference between the nine-year-old Suleiman and his older self when they are narrating? What language choices enable Matar to differentiate these two voices?

CHAPTER-BY-CHAPTER ANALYSIS

Chapter 1 (pp.1–9)

Summary: *Najwa is 'ill' during the night; the following morning she takes Suleiman to town and buys him treats; he sees his father, who is supposedly away, in the square; on the way home they are followed by a Revolutionary Committee car.*

The first chapter introduces us to the central relationship in the novel: Najwa and Suleiman's mother–son relationship. We are told in the first two sentences that this is Tripoli in the summer of 1979, but few facts in the rest of the novel will be so concrete, explicit, clear or certain. This is partly because in these early sentences, the voice is that of Suleiman as an adult, 'recalling ... that ... summer' (p.1). By the end of this first page, however, the narrative voice has become that of the nine-year-old Suleiman during that summer. This voice remains the dominant narrative voice for the novel, with occasional exceptions when the adult Suleiman intrudes, observing, for example, the effect of a particular incident on his adult life.

The child voice, unlike the adult voice, is often unclear or incomplete regarding details, and information is often conveyed to us through subtext rather than text. A strong example in this first chapter is Suleiman's discussion of his mother's 'illness'. In later chapters we will come to realise that in fact she is drunk rather than ill but, to begin with, we understand the situation through the partial comprehension of a child. When she takes Suleiman to town and buys him treats, the implication is that she is showing her repentance for her behaviour the night before. This is a regular pattern which follows her drinking sessions, but Suleiman is not yet quite aware of this: he simply observes that 'on such mornings she was always generous and embarrassed' (p.3).

Similarly, when Suleiman sees Baba (who is supposed to be away on a business trip) in the square with his clerk Nasser, he seems to recognise that something is wrong but is unable to understand or correctly attribute it: 'I felt sick, anxious that I had somehow done the wrong thing' (p.6).

This chapter also introduces the importance of religion and prayer in the novel. Suleiman mentions the Quran on the second page; he recalls his mother's blessing for Baba when he left, 'May God bring you back safely ... and make your trip profitable' (p.5); and when the Revolutionary Committee car follows them, Suleiman prays.

Q What do we learn about Suleiman's personality and character in this first chapter?

Q How much do we learn about the setting (social, political, geographical) of the novel in the first chapter?

Chapter 2 (pp.10–21)

Summary: *Suleiman is woken in the middle of the night by Najwa, who is drunk; she tells him about the past and her marriage; the next day they visit Signor Il Calzoni's restaurant; she makes Suleiman promise to keep her stories secret; she buys more 'medicine' from the baker.*

We see again how Suleiman is forced to care for his mother when his father is away; he feels that he is able, and expected, to be responsible for her wellbeing. He describes both the comfort and the fear that this brings him: 'I worried how the world might change if even for a second I was to look away', yet he also reveals that 'her illness bound us into an intimacy that has since occupied the innermost memory I have of love'. He acknowledges that 'There was anger ... even ... hate, but always love' (p.21) and dreams of saving her (p.12): a fantasy that recurs throughout the novel.

We also learn some of Najwa's history – the story she tells him over and over when she is 'ill'. She describes how, desperate to avoid the arranged marriage, she took pills that 'made a woman no good' because 'who would want to remain married to a woman who couldn't bear children?' (p.12). She recounts her fear of the consummation of the marriage, which led to her fainting and remembering nothing of losing her virginity.

Key point

This is an important example of the way in which the novel tells a story without directly explaining what has happened. We know from the 'bloodstained handkerchief' her parents remove from the bedroom that the event has occurred, and, as she says to Suleiman, 'Nine months later I had you' (p.14). This is typical of the style of Matar's narrative. There is no doubt as to what has happened, but there is never a mention of 'sex' or even a euphemism. We are left to draw our own conclusions from the carefully planted (though in this case very obvious) clues.

At the conclusion of the chapter, Suleiman briefly slips into his adult voice to describe 'what I then could only explain as her illness' (p.21) – another example of how the novel gives us information in a succinct way without interrupting the narrative. For the rest of the book he continues to refer to his mother's 'medicine' and her 'illness', even though we now recognise it as a reliance on alcohol as a coping mechanism.

Q How does Matar make us realise that the 'illness' is actually drunkenness?

Chapter 3 (pp.22–41)

Summary: *Kareem learns to drive; Kareem and Suleiman visit Lepcis with Rashid and his students; Suleiman recalls an incident when his father imported cows and Um Masoud complained – we discover through this that Ustath Jafer is with the Mokhabarat; Rashid is taken; Suleiman tries to rebuild his friendship with Kareem.*

The trip to Lepcis (one of few events set away from the house) gives Suleiman, and readers, a glimpse into the world beyond his confined existence. Although it is a short section in the chapter, it presents a microcosm illustrating several key aspects of his experiences of life.

Suleiman is invigorated by the university students' energy and knowledge of the world. Although he is initially nervous and reluctant to go – as he waves goodbye to his mother he says 'I felt a string in my heart break' (p.25) – he enjoys and seems enlivened by the trip with Kareem and his father. He is envious of Kareem and Rashid's closeness and even affection, and we know already that his relationship with his own father is not so simple. (His discussion of his father following the visit to Lepcis compares Baba and Rashid, offering us an insight into Suleiman and Baba's relationship.) He is also besotted with an erotic fresco of a Maenad, and kisses her image when nobody is looking.

Shortly afterwards, Suleiman and Kareem watch two of the university students embracing under the trees. Later, the male student is involved in a fight and Kareem and Suleiman 'weren't sure if it was over the girl' (p.28). The fight is a reminder that violence is omnipresent in the lives of Libyans at this time, and it is related calmly, foreshadowing several instances of Suleiman's own casual violence later in the novel.

His responses to these issues (education, family bonding, love, sex and violence) remind us that although Suleiman is young and naive about both the political world and the personal, he is also poised on the edge of an understanding of these things; perhaps he is travelling towards 'the country of men'.

The other key incident in this chapter is Rashid's arrest. Suleiman describes the incident in detail, but with little emotion (pp.35–6). However, elsewhere he hints that it affected him deeply: he says seeing it happen 'made my belly swim' (p.33). It is one thing to see interrogations on television, but quite another when it happens to his neighbour, right in front of him. Before relating Rashid's arrest, Suleiman describes how the neighbourhood children are amusing themselves: 'traitors' had printed and distributed leaflets criticising the Guide and the Revolutionary Committees, and the children have been throwing them into people's gardens. Suleiman shows little understanding of the importance of these leaflets, which, we later discover, Rashid, Baba, Moosa, Nasser and the students had probably printed.

Q Kareem says, 'Children are useless in a war' (p.27). What understanding do the children in *In the Country of Men* have of their country's political situation?

Q Why does Suleiman describe the removal of Rashid with such unemotional detail?

Chapter 4 (pp.42–51)

Summary: *Baba returns home from his 'business trip'; Suleiman climbs the mulberry tree in the garden, gorges on mulberries, and spends so long in the sun that he becomes fevered and faints.*

In this chapter we see how Suleiman feels free to be a child again once Baba is home. Although all is not well in the world (the family are worried about Rashid), for Suleiman there is relief that he is no longer 'the man of the house' (p.5), responsible for his mother. He feels secure in the knowledge that 'everything can be normal again' and he 'can leave the house without worrying' (p.45). While his parents are having the traditional afternoon nap, which he never manages, he climbs a ladder to the mulberry tree overhanging from Rashid's garden. He spends too long in the sun, stuffing himself full of berries and reflecting on teachings of the Quran, until eventually he begins to suffer from a sunstroke fever and faints.

It is almost as though Suleiman is so glad to be relieved of the responsibility of caring for his mother that he temporarily even loses the ability to care for himself. Surely a boy who had grown up in the desert heat of Libya would know better than to stay in the sun so long: perhaps he was simply revelling in the joy of having no responsibility, or subconsciously wanting someone to be responsible for *him*.

Q What does Najwa mean when she tells Faraj he has 'chosen a dead-end road' (p.43)?

Chapter 5 (pp.52–60)

Summary: *Suleiman wakes from his fever to hear Mama and Moosa discussing Rashid and the pamphlets; Suleiman gets up to talk with Moosa, and thinks about how Moosa has often read poetry to him; the three of them eat; there's a knock at the door.*

Although he doesn't engage in it, Suleiman overhears a conversation that gives us concrete information about the political activities Rashid, Baba and their associates are involved in. Moosa is excited that the students at the university have been mobilised by the leaflets and are beginning to object to '*the extremes of the revolution*' (pp.52–3). He says, 'These are exciting times. Everything can change' (p.53). Najwa, on the other hand, calls the students 'foolish dreamers' (p.53): she is fearful and wishes that her husband were not involved. She has seen what happened to Rashid and she worries that the same will happen to Faraj. This fear foreshadows what eventually does occur.

They don't know where Baba is – Moosa says he's 'lying low' after the events with Rashid (p.52). They comfort themselves by eating together, and Suleiman wishes Moosa would take him to Baba's study to read to him; he remembers poems Moosa has read before, and we see a love of literature that they share. This will be echoed later when Suleiman rescues one of Baba's books (in Chapter 8): books represent all the things Suleiman respects about his father.

Q Why does Suleiman make up a happy dream to tell his mother?

Chapter 6 (pp.61–9)

Summary: *Members of the Revolutionary Committee arrive in search of Baba and Suleiman overhears their conversation with Moosa and Mama; Moosa charms them while Mama makes them tea; after they leave, Moosa refuses to tell Mama in front of Suleiman what they said.*

We are reminded again of Suleiman's youth, innocence and inexperience. When he hears the Committee men arrive at the house, he wonders: 'How many of them were there, hundreds, thousands?' (p.61). However, imagery that he later uses is sophisticated and complex.

Consider, for example, his thoughts when he imagines his mother a heroine in a film (pp.65–6). Phrases such as 'an infinite intimacy is born, a trust unbound and unhindered by the possibility of betrayal' (p.66) are not the thoughts of a nine-year-old boy; instead, this is a moment where the adult Suleiman's voice creeps into the narration, although here (unlike in other instances) he does not acknowledge it by referring to his adulthood. Instead the narrative carries on uninterrupted and we feel the young Suleiman's quiet bafflement as Moosa refuses to discuss the incident in front of him.

Q How does Suleiman convey to us the characters and intentions of the Committee members?

Chapter 7 (pp.70–83)

Summary: *Suleiman is sent to practise the piano; Moosa and Mama clean up after the Committee visit; Suleiman ponders the history of Moosa and Baba's friendship and some of Moosa's business ventures; Mama becomes angry with Suleiman; he goes to bed and Moosa massages him.*

In this chapter we begin to see the toll that Rashid's arrest and Baba's absence are having on the characters. Suleiman senses the changed atmosphere particularly keenly: 'I longed for how things had been' (p.73). He feels angry but can't identify the source of his anger; Mama's crying only increases his anger. Although he is not able to articulate it, it seems that her heightened vulnerability and helplessness in this situation frighten and anger him. Although he is accustomed to seeing her in a weakened state (when she is 'ill'), her 'illness' has a predictability and familiarity that this situation lacks.

When Mama discovers that Suleiman had wet himself in fear when the Committee members were in the house, she is angry instead of sympathetic. For both Mama and Suleiman, then, vulnerability leads to anger. They are both out of their comfort zones and unable to fix things, so instead they lash out at each other. Moosa provides a calm buffer between them, but even he is vulnerable, and despite Suleiman's deep fondness and regard for him, Moosa is powerless to bring the boy comfort. The chapter ends with a silent Suleiman withdrawing from Moosa's caring bedtime massage, unable 'to be normal again, to laugh and play with him' (p.83).

Q How would you describe Suleiman and Moosa's relationship?

Chapter 8 (pp.84–100)

Summary: *Suleiman wakes up in Mama's bed, and ruminates on his parents' sleeping habits; he recalls once seeing his parents having sex; Mama and Moosa hang a portrait of the Guide in the reception room and burn Baba's books; Suleiman rescues one of the books; Moosa and Mama argue about the resistance.*

In one of the longer chapters of the novel, Suleiman's thoughts turn to his parents' relationship. He again reveals the limitations of his youth: his attention to detail is careful and his observations meticulous, yet he seems unable to integrate the information into a thorough understanding of the situation.

For example, Suleiman notices that when Baba is home, his mother often sleeps on the couch, claiming that her husband snores. Suleiman seems to doubt the claim and says that he 'always suspected there was a different reason' (p.87). He even explores a memory of seeing his parents having sex, noting that Mama seemed unhappy. But he doesn't clearly make the connection between these two facts. He does ponder whether he should have been somehow able to put a stop to 'something that the angels I was certain never blessed, something that made Mama leave her bed every night to sleep on the sofa' (p.88), but is left with no resolution, no understanding of the complexities of an adult relationship and a marriage. His desire to rescue his mother, though, is an idea that recurs throughout the novel.

The other important section in this chapter is the burning of Baba's books. In another example of his youthful naivety, Suleiman fails to understand the reasons behind Mama and Moosa's actions. He feels that they are betraying Baba, who loves his books dearly, and by extension somehow betraying Suleiman himself. This is not helped by the fact that they have just replaced a photograph of Baba in the reception room with a portrait of the Guide – for Suleiman, they seem to be attacking Baba from all directions. When Suleiman follows the adults outside, he finds that they are not only preparing to burn Baba's books, but they are doing so in Suleiman's own tin bucket. The betrayal seems even more hurtful, and he decides to secretly keep a book (*Democracy Now*) that they had dropped on their way. Through all this, he doesn't recognise that their actions are motivated by a desire to protect Baba.

Key point

Although Mama and Moosa argue about Baba's involvement in the resistance movement, they both share a desire to live in a 'better Libya' (p.96). They are simply unable to agree upon how to achieve this.

Q Why does Najwa criticise Moosa and the efforts of the resistance movement?

Chapter 9 (pp.101–10)

Summary: *Baba returns; after talking with Moosa he packs his things and leaves; Suleiman hides the book* Democracy Now *in his room; he plays with Kareem and they have an argument.*

Suleiman is happy to have his father home and still doesn't understand the gravity of the situation. He is puzzled when Baba commends Mama and Moosa for burning his books and, although he doesn't fully comprehend why, he realises that it is important to hide the book he rescued.

For the first time since Rashid was taken, Suleiman goes to play with Kareem. Other boys from the neighbourhood join them and soon the once-close friends are fighting. Suleiman says things he knows will hurt Kareem – making comments about Rashid's disappearance, for example – as well as using careless childish insults like 'crybaby' (p.110). He seems unsure of why he is hurting his friend, but he is unable to prevent himself 'feeling a dark, unstoppable force gain momentum' (p.108). Although most of his quarrel with Kareem is verbal, we see a capacity for cruelty in him, which is later fulfilled in his behaviour towards Bahloul.

Q Why do you think the boys fight with each other in this chapter?

Chapter 10 (pp.111–19)

Summary: *Mama, Moosa and Suleiman await the Committee members, who don't arrive; Suleiman judges himself for how he behaved with Kareem; he sees Rashid's interrogation on television and then pours Mama's 'medicine' down the sink; Suleiman lets Bahloul into the house but then chases him out, throwing stones at him.*

Suleiman's guilt and regret about his argument with his good friend play out as a dialogue in his mind, with voices attacking and criticising him. (This happens later, too, after Suleiman visits the wounded Baba in darkness; see pp.201–2.) The voices even accuse him of being a 'traitor' (p.113). This is a very loaded word, echoing the political situation and the world in which Suleiman is becoming a man: a world where loyalty and betrayal can mean life or death.

He watches Rashid's interrogation on television alone while his mother has her afternoon nap. This is typical of Suleiman's experience: despite his closeness with his mother, he is often alone in the world and much of the narrative rests on his own internal observations, memories and assessments of the world. It is fitting, then, that there is nobody with whom he might share this experience.

Suleiman lets Bahloul the beggar into the house, offering him food, but when Bahloul finds the empty 'medicine' bottle, he leaves. Suleiman runs after him, throwing rocks and taking an unexpected pleasure in the power of scaring someone.

Q Although there is no explicit link between the interrogation and Suleiman's treatment of Bahloul, do you think Matar is making a comment on the influence of television over children's behaviour?

Chapter 11 (pp.120–33)

Summary: *Najwa orders more alcohol from the baker; Suleiman has his first daytime nap; while playing outside with the boys, Suleiman talks with Sharief in the car; he refuses to tell his mother what they said.*

Suleiman has never been able to sleep in the daytime, as is the tradition in the hot Libyan climate. For the first time he manages to sleep in the afternoon, but when he wakes it is to discover that Mama has left the gas on in the kitchen. He is furious with her, not least because she blames *him* for the error, and shuts himself in his room for a time. Even her attempt at a lighthearted reconciliation – a note whose contents are directly appropriated from Suleiman's favourite story, 'Scheherazade' – falls flat and he maintains his anger as long as he can.

Eventually he tires of his protest and goes outside to play, but most of the boys seem to have sided with Kareem and they run away from Suleiman.

Key point

The only boy to show any real friendliness to Suleiman is Adnan, who even tries to 'comfort' Suleiman (p.128). This isolated kindness increases the impact of Suleiman's accidental cruelty to Adnan in Chapter 15.

Suleiman then goes to the car in which Sharief is sitting and they talk. Although Suleiman knows Sharief is lying when he claims to be a friend of Baba's, he is somehow drawn to the man. He recalls that, on the night when the Committee men came to their house, Sharief found the 'medicine' bottle but chose not to pursue the issue, even though alcohol is both illegal and against religious strictures. Sharief uses this as a bribe to get information out of Suleiman, claiming it will help Baba, and Suleiman feels himself caught in a moral conundrum he is too young to understand: he knows Sharief is manipulating him but is compelled to do what he believes will protect his father.

Q What is the significance of Suleiman napping during the day for the first time?

Chapter 12 (pp.134–41)

Summary: *Suleiman tells Mama about talking to Sharief; Nasser's father rings to blame Faraj for Nasser's involvement in the resistance; Nasser calls and speaks on a tapped line to Suleiman; the interlocutor then phones Suleiman directly and asks for Nasser's address.*

Chapter 12 reveals the extent of control that the Guide and the Revolutionary Committee have over the lives of Libyans – particularly those suspected of traitorous activity. Suleiman and Mama are very familiar with their line being tapped and even know how to tell, from the echo in the phone, whether someone is listening in. This chapter also reiterates Suleiman's vulnerability and childishness: although he feels an unprecedented affection for Nasser, he still willingly offers up Nasser's address when asked to by the voice on the phone.

Q Why do you think Suleiman is willing to give out Nasser's address?

Chapter 13 (pp.142–9)

Summary: *Suleiman reflects on his parents' relationship and how his mother views the men in her life; he recalls the story she has told so often, of her arranged marriage, this time including details of some of her siblings including her brother Khaled; Suleiman dreams of rescuing his mother from her past.*

Here we see the influence of Mama's story on Suleiman's thoughts. She has told him the story so often when she is 'ill' that he even begins to retell it to himself when he is alone. He entertains fantasies of somehow being able to rescue his mother when she was young, preventing all her misery to come. He longs to at last become a man: 'not to do all the things normally associated with manhood ... but to ... rescue that girl from her black day' (p.148).

Q How does this chapter address the notion of betrayal?

Chapter 14 (pp.150–6)

Summary: *Nasser visits with his daughter Siham; Suleiman falls in love with her but she holds his father responsible for bringing 'ruin' on her brother's head.*

Suleiman's memory of once betraying a fellow schoolboy is juxtaposed in this chapter with his sudden and naive affection for Siham – whom he knows is too close to his age for them to be a legitimate romantic match when they are older. The idea of betrayal is explored both through Siham's accusations of Baba's role in Nasser's downfall and through Suleiman's behaviour towards his schoolmate. He compares the two and feels shame at his betrayals. This episode is then contrasted with that involving Sharief at the end of the chapter, as Suleiman observes him sitting in his car, 'loyal to his cause' (p.156).

Q 'Loyalty' is usually seen as an admirable trait. What is the effect of using this word with reference to the man who took Rashid and attempted to take Baba?

Chapter 15 (pp.157–64)

Summary: *Mama and Suleiman visit Ustath Jafer and Um Masoud with cake and a plea for help; Suleiman wants to play with the boys but accidentally hits Adnan with a rock; Sharief intervenes to stop Suleiman and Osama fighting.*

We see Najwa's desperation when she goes to the Mokhabarat for help to get Baba home alive. Previously she has avoided contact with Um Masoud, but in this chapter she humbles herself and takes cake to her, knowing that Ustath Jafer may be able to help Faraj survive what he is undergoing.

Key point

This chapter contains a notable example of the intrusion of the adult-Suleiman's voice: when he analyses the impact of this visit to Um Masoud, he recognises that when he must deal with authority in his adult life he still feels the echoes of that visit and its attendant shame, submission and deprecation. He also links this with an aspect of his faith, noting that in prayer he experiences similar feelings.

Wanting to join in with the boys' games and hoping to impress them with his aim, Suleiman accidentally hits Adnan, who suffers from a form of haemophilia. The boys turn against Suleiman in anger and Osama even physically attacks him. It is Sharief who comes to his rescue, telling the boys that 'they can't just hit each other over nothing' (p.164). It is unexpected that Sharief, an agent of distress to not only Kareem's but also Suleiman's family, won't tolerate the boys' fighting and violence.

Q What techniques does Matar employ to convey to us Najwa's feelings about going to Ustath Jafer for help?

Chapter 16 (pp.165–75)

Summary: *Adnan is taken away in an ambulance; Suleiman decides to bring* Democracy Now *and the names of Baba's associates to Sharief but finds him gone; Mama is 'ill' and for the first time, Suleiman asks her to tell him the stories of her past; she tells him in detail about her punishments as a child for socialising with boys; Suleiman fantasises again about rescuing her.*

There is instability and change in Suleiman's life, reflecting the political and social volatility around him. We see examples in this and the previous chapter, including the following:

- Something Suleiman has previously resented (his mother's stories when she is 'ill') becomes a comfort to him, and he actively seeks it.
- Sharief, an enemy to Rashid and Baba, becomes a kind of hero by rescuing Suleiman.
- Kareem and Suleiman's friendship seems lost for good.

The stories of Najwa's past are detailed and vivid in this chapter, including descriptions of the punishments her family subjected her to for misdemeanours such as being seen in mixed company in public at age fourteen. This chapter gives us an insight into the strict life of a traditional family in Libya at this time, and the restrictions a young woman faced. The punishments Najwa endured provide a parallel for the other forms of violence in the book – including beatings during interrogations and Suleiman's almost unthinking violence against Bahloul.

Chapter 17 (pp.176–88)

Summary: *Suleiman tries again to give the book and names to Sharief but he's uninterested; Mama, Moosa and Suleiman watch the televised execution of Rashid.*

Much of the novel comprises static, slow and domestic scenes, reported through Suleiman's interior monologue. This chapter provides contrast and one of the most visceral and violent scenes in the novel, and yet this scene – that of Rashid's execution – is mediated by the television: we are still not observing direct action, but watching the event at a distance. Although the lead-up and the execution itself are confronting and described in great detail, the action takes place far away from Suleiman's house – the centre of his world – where the novel is concentrated.

Q Why do you think Suleiman, Mama and Moosa are compelled to relive the confronting event immediately afterwards?

Chapter 18 (pp.189–97)

Summary: *It rains for the first time in the novel; Mama farewells Salma and Kareem but Suleiman refuses to; Um Masoud brings good news about Baba and Moosa goes to fetch him; Mama covers all the mirrors and Suleiman isn't allowed to see Baba yet.*

This chapter illustrates, with a concrete event, a narrative device Matar uses throughout: that of obscuring the facts and yet revealing information in other ways. Here, the facts are Baba's trauma and injury. When Baba returns home, Suleiman does not see him at first. He hears 'Moosa's voice struggle under a heavy weight' (p.194), and then hears them enter Mama and Baba's room. Although we are not told Moosa is carrying Baba, it is clearly so. It is equally clear, a moment later, that the 'dark brown spots' on Moosa's shirt are Baba's blood, even though Moosa tries to cover the fact, claiming he had lost a tooth (p.194). Mama also tries to conceal the facts, explaining that Suleiman cannot see Baba yet because he is 'not feeling well' and is 'resting' (p.194).

From all these details we realise, although Suleiman may not yet, that Baba is terribly wounded and has probably been beaten or tortured. The symbolism of hidden facts is extended when Suleiman discovers the white sheets over the mirrors. Not only does Baba not want his son to see his injuries, but also he himself cannot face them, and he tries to erase the facts by hiding them with a blank, white sheet. This only heightens our awareness of the horror of what must have occurred. Matar harnesses his readers' imagination to increase the impact of the events: because the extent of Baba's injuries has no boundaries in our imagination, and Matar's words impose none, the injuries take on epic proportions.

This is contrasted, in the final section of the chapter (pp.196–7), with Suleiman's reflections on hope, heroism and the loss of innocence. These ideas are considered with reference to cowboy films Suleiman has seen, where the facts and details are concrete, visible and unambiguous. The execution, too, is concrete and stamped into Suleiman's memory: his observation of this makes us grateful that he has not yet witnessed tangible evidence of his father's experience and injuries.

Chapter 19 (pp.198–203)

Summary: *Suleiman wakes late and feels angry that Mama will not tell him the full story about Baba; she realises it is important for Suleiman to see Baba and takes him into the bedroom but in darkness; Suleiman goes outside, unsatisfied, and glimpses Baba through the window; Baba is horrified and refuses to see him.*

There is a tension in this incident between Suleiman's desire to know all the facts and his inability to handle the situation. He knows that he is not being told the truth about Baba and his parents' attempts to protect him leave him unfulfilled. However, when he does peek through the window and finally sees Baba, he is horrified by the image, physically winded and 'full of fear' (p.202). Being treated as a child frustrates him, but he is not ready yet to accept the traumas and responsibilities associated with being an adult.

This chapter also reveals Baba's shame and pain at having been beaten. He can't bear for his son to see him and is dealing with not only his physical injuries, but also the psychological impact of the trauma he has been through.

Chapter 20 (pp.204–12)

Summary: *Moosa visits to talk with Baba; Moosa and Mama argue about the resistance; Moosa reveals that he and his father are being deported; Suleiman begins to bond again with Baba, taking him up to the roof and trying to feed him mulberries.*

The discussion between Moosa and Mama (pp.207–8) offers us an important illustration of the political state of the country and the challenges the resistance movement faces. This is one of few detailed discussions of such facts.

The argument between Mama and Moosa parallels their discussion in Chapter 8 (pp.95–8). In the first, it is Mama who is afraid of the resistance: scornful of Moosa's involvement and resentful of Baba's. In the second, here, Mama is a little more sympathetic to her husband and Rashid, although she still says she didn't support the movement: 'they weren't standing for me' (p.208). Moosa, however, has changed. He is disillusioned about the resistance and the events of recent days have filled him with despair about the state of the country.

Baba chooses this moment to rise from bed and reconnect with Suleiman. They go outside together but Baba can't eat the mulberries Suleiman offers him (pp.211–12). There is a symbolic explanation for this. Suleiman tells Baba he thinks that the angels brought mulberries to earth from heaven, 'to make life easier for us' (p.211). (This is a theory Suleiman previously proposed to Moosa, p.59.) But in his present state, and after what he has recently seen and undergone, Baba literally cannot stomach Suleiman's childish fantasy of an easier life. Baba's only response to Suleiman is to show him where the Revolutionaries extinguished their cigarettes against his head (p.212): this suggests he is focused on what has happened, and he is unable to indulge in the optimism his son is attempting to draw him into.

Q What does Moosa mean when he describes 'the betrayal in [Baba's] eyes' (p.207)?

Chapter 21 (pp.213–19)

Summary: *Two weeks on, Baba turns a corner in his recovery; Suleiman walks to the sea to swim; he sees Bahloul there, frightens him into jumping into the water, and, when Bahloul begins to drown, accelerates the process instead of rescuing him.*

The chapter begins optimistically but ends with a scene of cruelty and possibly even death. (It is not explicitly stated whether Bahloul lives or dies, but Suleiman leaves him clinging to a pier post, unable to swim and with no apparent help at hand. The narrative thus leaves the reader uncertain about Bahloul's fate.) Baba has begun to recover and Mama, too, has regained some optimism and quality of life, as evidenced by her desire to go outside and draw. This is an unprecedented activity within the timeframe of the book, and it is clearly positive, constructive and creative, where previously her self-medicating has been destructive and negative.

And yet, despite the optimism, when Suleiman inadvertently places Bahloul's life in danger, he barely tries to rectify his error. Although he says 'I wanted to save him', he doesn't know how, and instead, 'without deciding to', he pushes Bahloul further underwater with his foot and kicks him (p.218). This scene is as graphic as the earlier execution, and perhaps more disturbing because there seems little motivation for Suleiman's violence.

It is significant that after Suleiman's cruelty towards Bahloul he longs for the friend he has lost in Kareem. He is so alone, confused about the world and unhappy that he has become someone capable of cruelty and (perhaps) even murder.

Q Do you think that Bahloul survives or drowns? What evidence in the text supports your answer?

Chapter 22 (pp.220–3)

Summary: *Suleiman again witnesses his parents having sex; they tell him he's going to visit Cairo.*

During this short chapter, we see how a renewed – or perhaps, more correctly, a *new* – sense of love and companionship between Mama and Baba coincides with a sense of dissatisfaction and even distress for Suleiman. He feels a 'quiet anger'; is 'nervous' and 'anxious' (p.220); has abstract bad dreams (p.221); longs 'for the first time ever' to go back to school (p.221) and is frightened of the dark outside (p.222). When, on top of this, his parents tell him they are sending him to Egypt to 'visit' Moosa and see the pyramids (p.223), he is distraught and does not want to go.

Suleiman has plenty of reasons for his discomfort. He has recently witnessed a number of traumatic events (including the interrogation and execution of Rashid, his father's injuries and the incident with Bahloul) and has not had or sought sufficient support to cope with the after-effects of these experiences. Also, and perhaps more importantly within the context of the narrative, he has suddenly lost his place as primary comfort to his mother and is no longer the main focus of her attention.

His parents' happiness with each other is new to him, and he is forced to reconsider his own value, purpose and place in the world. His mother no longer needs him by her side and is therefore less available to him, as we see when she sends him back to his own bed after he wakes up from a nightmare (p.221). Dealing with this new identity is a challenge.

Q How does Matar convey to the reader, without ever stating it, that the 'visit' to Cairo will not be a short-term stay?

Chapter 23 (pp.224–32)

Summary: *Baba and Mama drive Suleiman to the airport; he arrives in Cairo and gradually integrates into Egyptian life; years pass while he remains an expatriate and an 'evader' (p.230); he becomes a pharmacist; he begins to mourn his loss of a homeland.*

This is the only chapter during which years pass – elsewhere in the novel (and in the early part of this chapter) time moves slowly as the narrative explores the events of a single summer. This emphasises the fact that the summer of 1979 was one of the most significant of Suleiman's life. In earlier chapters he has told, in great detail, of his inner thought processes during the minutes, hours, days and months surrounding Rashid's execution and his father's incarceration and torture. Here, years of activity are compressed into single paragraphs and Suleiman skips over many details, including his own feelings.

The exception to this is the end of the chapter, when he discusses the psychological effects of living as an 'evader' from his country. Although he has come to feel 'free ... from Libya' and to appreciate that liberation (p.230), he also suffers 'an ever-present absence (p.231), a 'void' and an 'emptiness' (p.232) that come from having lost his homeland. He notes 'Egypt has not replaced Libya' (p.232).

Key point

This chapter contains an event which 'bookends' the novel: Mama's purchase of the sesame sticks for Suleiman in the market. In the first instance (p.3) they amuse him and he takes advantage of Mama's guilty repentance; here, his distress is too great to be overcome with treats.

Chapter 24 (pp.233–43)

Summary: *Suleiman reports the horrific financial strains placed upon those still in Libya; Baba gets a new job and also begins translating Machiavelli; Baba is arrested and Mama becomes 'ill' once more; Suleiman rejects Kareem's attempt to rekindle their friendship; Baba dies; Siham and Kareem are engaged.*

Here we see Suleiman gradually embracing his life away from Libya and refusing to reconnect with his past. He withdraws from his mother when she turns to drinking after Baba's arrest, refusing to answer her calls. Nor will he reply to Kareem's heartfelt letter. Fifteen years after Suleiman's exile, when the ban on Libyans travelling is lifted, he is excited about the possibility of seeing his parents, but is 'cruelly' denied this: his father dies just days later (p.239).

Q How is the young adult Suleiman different from the child? What characteristics have remained the same?

Chapter 25 (pp.244–5)

Summary: *Suleiman waits at the bus station for Mama to arrive in Alexandria.*

The book concludes with this very short chapter, in which Suleiman and his mother are reunited after so many years. It is fitting that the central relationship in the book – between mother and son – is the focus of the final few pages, just as it was the focus of the opening pages. It is also fitting that the final sentence, which describes the moment when she arrives, is concrete and lacks explicit sentiment, and yet with it Matar manages to create a subtext full of emotion.

Q What do you think the first things Suleiman and his mother say to each other might be? (Think about what you know of the characters' personalities, and the journey each has taken throughout the novel.)

CHARACTERS & RELATIONSHIPS

Suleiman

Key quotes

'Take care of your mother. You are the man of the house now …' (p.5)

'… doubtful of the world and my place in it …' (p.21)

'I wondered what it would be like to slap a man …' (p.71)

Although Suleiman tells the story from his perspective as an adult, many years later, the primary voice of the narrator is that of the nine-year-old Suleiman. The adult voice occasionally enters the narrative to give an explanation of how an event from that summer impacted on his later life.

He teeters between childhood and adulthood, understanding the world around him with varying degrees of depth. He's both sensitive and violent; often solitary; looks up to but feels distanced from his father; adores and is frustrated by his mother. He is named for Suleiman the

Magnificent (a successful emperor in the Ottoman Empire), a suggestion from his uncle Khaled (p.145).

We witness all of the events in the novel through Suleiman's perspective, and Matar expects us to align our sympathies with him. But Suleiman is not a 'hero' or even innocent. He is violent, hurting his friends as well as Bahloul the beggar, and he tries to offer Sharief information which will ultimately implicate and endanger family friends, such as Moosa, about whom he cares deeply.

Although it could be argued that Suleiman has simply fallen for Sharief's lies that this information will help Faraj, it is also clear that he knows Sharief is not always telling the truth. Perhaps Matar expects us to forgive Suleiman because he is still a child and struggles to understand the full truth of any situation. Or perhaps he wants us to understand that even 'good' characters, people we believe in and care about, can do 'bad' things; no-one is perfect and humans are inherently flawed.

Domestic or political?

Is the novel about a young boy's home life against a backdrop of political unrest, or is it a story of contemporary Libyan history told through a young boy's perspective? Which is more important for you when you read the novel? Both of these storylines are central and both are focused through Suleiman's character. His relationship with his mother and father; his transition from youth towards manhood and the influence his friends and his parents' friends have on his life are all explored in the novel. And yet the political and social state of Libya ten years into Qaddafi's rule is also of central concern, and we learn of this situation through Suleiman's highly subjective and restricted understanding.

Q If you were in Suleiman's situation, how do you think you would respond? Would you speak to Sharief? How would you feel about caring for your mother when she was 'ill'?

Najwa (Mama)

Key quotes

'Nothing angered Mama more than the story of Scheherazade ... Scheherazade was a coward who accepted slavery over death.' (p.15)

'If love starts somewhere ... for me that person was her.' (p.21)

'But no, I must be a good wife, loyal and unquestioning, support my man regardless. I'll support nothing that puts my son in danger.' (p.97)

'The mother who tried to never have me, the mother who never chose it, the mother who resisted in all the ways she knew how.' (p.245)

Najwa, or Mama, is a central figure in *In the Country of Men*. She is the most important person in Suleiman's life during the summer of 1979, and while he is resentful of her 'illness' (her drunkenness, which occurs only when Baba is away), he adores her and rarely strays far from the house. His ambivalence towards her is evidenced when he imagines life without her and isn't sure whether he is feeling 'fear or excitement ... at the thought of losing her' (p.17). This indicates that there are several sides to her character: the positive traits, for which her son loves her, and the negative, for which he resents her. She shows two versions of herself when she is 'ill' – the needy, dangerous one, and, the next morning, a repentant and remorseful one who seeks to spoil and please Suleiman as a way of apologising.

Najwa herself is aware of some of the conflicts in her personality. For example, early in the novel she tells Suleiman how she tried to make herself unable to bear children, as a defence against an arranged marriage with an unknown older man. She took pills (which failed) and still describes her marriage as a 'black day' (p.11, p.144, p.146) and yet acknowledges that Suleiman is one of the best things to have happened to her: she says to him, 'You are my miracle' (p.12).

A significant change occurs for Najwa in Chapter 21, when Faraj's health begins to turn a corner two weeks after his return home. Instead of being upset by his wounds, she finds a new positivity in life. Where in the past she has done her duty as a wife – done the right thing and supported him even though she did not support the resistance – now she seems genuinely uplifted by his presence. She is re-inspired to draw and she sings as she goes about her housework, feeling optimistic and cheerful. Her new outlook is perhaps the result of having Faraj safe at home and no longer capable of participating in the resistance movement. She begins to have a genuine affection for, and connection with, her husband (as we realise when Suleiman sees them having sex, p.221). This new relationship leaves little room for Suleiman, since his father is always home and his mother is now never 'ill'.

Fear

Fear seems to motivate a number of Najwa's decisions and behaviours. We see how she abandons what was a very close friendship with Salma after Rashid is taken, for fear of associating with the family of someone who is now officially regarded as a traitor. She also acts out of fear when she goes to Ustath Jafer and Um Masoud, effectively begging for mercy on her husband's life. One of the reasons she doesn't support the resistance is fear; not wanting to risk her own or her family's life she would prefer 'walking beside the wall' (p.40) in order to stay unnoticed and safe. She sees only injury and loss resulting from the resistance movement's efforts, and she wants no part of it.

The past

Suleiman observes that for his mother, 'The only things that mattered were in the past' (p.11). Najwa is influenced by her distressing past, the events she repeatedly describes when telling her story to her son. Her brothers married her swiftly to Faraj because she had been caught socialising with a boy at age fourteen and her family were desperate to prevent shame being brought upon them by a dishonourable daughter. She relives, over and over, their punishments and her own fear at what was to happen:

> They didn't know how it felt waiting in that room, where the complete stranger who was now my husband was going to walk in alone and, without introduction, undress me and do filthy, revolting things. (p.12)

She appears to cling to the horror of this event, even while she enjoys Faraj's company and no longer detests him. Her drinking is always tied to her storytelling about this 'black day' (p.11, p.144, p.146) and the text suggests that it is her attempt to survive the trauma of her experience.

Q Do you think Najwa is a good mother to Suleiman? Why or why not? Support your answer with evidence from the text.

Faraj (Baba)

Key quotes

'At times I used to wish that Baba was more like Ustath Rashid.' (p.29)

'... although he was often serious, he very rarely became angry.' (p.38)

'He loves his books more than anything else.' (p.99)

'When he was home, Baba seemed distant.' (p.143)

Faraj is an educated, passionate, caring and determined man whose commitment to his political beliefs often leaves him distant from his family, and ultimately impacts on and endangers them. As a businessman he travels frequently, leaving behind his wife and young son, and instructing Suleiman to become the 'man of the house' (p.5) in his absence. Little does he know that while he is away his wife turns to alcohol for comfort, demanding a maturity of Suleiman that is perhaps beyond his years: he must provide not only practical but emotional support for her.

Although Faraj is usually known as 'Baba' in the novel, indicating that his identity is deeply tied up in his son's life, he has a parallel role in the novel as a member of the resistance movement against Qaddafi's rule. Two key moments in the narrative are when he returns after being held by the Revolutionary Committee and, just before he sends his son to Egypt, their embrace in the car. Both of these moments intricately connect Suleiman's life and the political world of the resistance movement.

Key point

As the above examples demonstrate, it is difficult to separate the two aspects of Faraj's character: his fatherhood and his politics.

Q How do you think Faraj would react if he found out about his wife's drinking?

Q Do you think Faraj is a good father to Suleiman? Why or why not?

Moosa

Key quotes

'At other times I secretly wished that Moosa, Baba's closest friend, was my father instead ... He often carried me on his shoulders to pick the high fruit, sweetened by the sun, on the crowns of the plum and orange trees in our garden.' (p.30)

'Moosa's laugh made you laugh even if you didn't find what he was laughing about funny.' (p.55)

'When Moosa read you had to stop and listen ...' (p.56)

Moosa, an old friend of Faraj's, is caring and compassionate, spending time with Suleiman and Najwa whenever Faraj is away. Suleiman looks up to him – even Najwa sees this and says 'I know how much you love him' (p.19). Moosa's affection towards Suleiman is consistent and uncomplicated, whereas Faraj's affection for him is sometimes distracted by his work and his political activities. Although Suleiman loves Baba, it is often Moosa who provides comfort and inspiration for him. For example, though Baba 'loves his books more than anything else' (p.99), it is Moosa who 'infected' Suleiman 'with his love of language' (p.58).

Although he is from Egypt, Moosa has embraced Libya as his homeland and is as passionate about the resistance movement as Faraj, Rashid, Nasser and the others. Mama accuses him of being a foreigner and says he should go back to his own country, but Moosa says, 'This is my country. I've lived here half of my life' (p.208). When he and his father receive a deportation notice, he is already disillusioned with the resistance movement and the treatment of those whom he loves. He returns to Egypt and provides a home for Suleiman when Faraj and Najwa send him to Cairo, away from the volatile situation in Libya.

Key point

Moosa's and Faraj's relationships with Suleiman can be directly contrasted. Whereas Moosa lifts Suleiman up, helping him reach the sweet fruits in life – both literally and through his passion for poetry and literature – Faraj is distant and Suleiman feels that when his father is reading, 'he was often busy ... and he would hardly notice me' (p.29).

Kareem

Key quotes

'... a certain sadness had entered his eyes the day Ustath Rashid was taken, but it wasn't the sadness of longing, it was the sadness of betrayal ...' (p.40)

Kareem and Suleiman are close friends, despite the three-year age difference between them, and Suleiman feels a camaraderie and closeness with Kareem that he rarely experiences anywhere else. However, after Rashid is taken, Najwa discourages the friendship – ostensibly because 'It just isn't good ... to be so close to all of his sadness' but really because she doesn't want her family to risk association with the family of a traitor (p.40). Suleiman longs to reconnect with his friend; he even wishes the Revolutionary Committee would return and take away his own father so he and Kareem could be 'equal, united again by that mysterious bond of blood' (p.41).

When this eventually happens, however, it does not rekindle the friendship. In fact Suleiman and Kareem never re-establish their trust and closeness. When Suleiman sees Kareem for the first time after Rashid's disappearance, he aches for their friendship and feels 'an infinite longing for nothing specific' (p.106), but is unable to express this and instead their meeting degenerates into a fight.

Although their last real contact is in a childish yet hurtful argument (pp.107–10), Kareem makes an effort, many years later, to contact Suleiman and renew their connection. In fact he makes a supreme effort: as he explains in his letter (pp.237–8), Najwa had refused to give him Suleiman's address in Cairo so he had to obtain it by underhand methods. This demonstrates Kareem's commitment to the friendship and his determination to repair the damage of the past.

Q Why do you think Suleiman is unable (or unwilling) to farewell Kareem when he leaves for Benghazi, and unable (or unwilling) to respond to his letter in Egypt?

Ustath Rashid

Key quotes

'No one knew why Ustath Rashid had been taken, but the next day the rumours began to spread that he had been a traitor.' (p.36)

'God knows if Rashid will make it, the poor man, stupid enough to believe your dreams.' (p.96)

Rashid, like Moosa, is someone Suleiman looks up to and admires. He is a loyal friend to Faraj – to the extent of lying to protect him during the public interrogation. Rashid is an educated man and although, as Suleiman observes, his professorship doesn't bring the family great wealth, he is deeply respected for his knowledge and his profession.

Rashid is one of the most morally unambiguous characters in the novel. Although we do not get to know him well, what we do see of him is energetic, modest, loyal, dedicated, caring and positive. He is friendly towards, and respected by, his students and is affectionate with his own son. Suleiman watches 'Kareem nuzzle into his father's side' on the bus home from Lepcis (p.29) and envies the easy closeness between the two.

Rashid also keeps his word to Faraj: he inscribed in a book he once gave as a gift to his friend the promise that he would be eternally loyal (p.105), and in the end he is. We never see Rashid behaving less than admirably, and his commendable qualities encourage us to empathise with him, increasing the tragedy of his arrest and his eventual execution.

Q Would you describe Rashid as heroic? Innocent? Why or why not?

Bahloul

Key quotes

'Although I knew Bahloul was mad, these words, these meaningless words that he always repeated, increased my confusion.' (p.49)

'... I smelled him and saw how dirty his jallabia was and how black his bare feet looked against the carpet.' (p.117)

A local beggar, Bahloul appears at several key moments of the story. He is present in the first chapter when Najwa takes Suleiman to town; in Chapter 4 when Suleiman steals the mulberries; in Chapter 10 when Suleiman watches the televised interrogation alone and in Chapter 21 when Suleiman attempts to drown him. Bahloul's frequent refrain is 'I see you, I see you' and Suleiman sometimes takes this to heart, considering the possible significance of the proclamation even though he knows Bahloul is mentally disturbed and the words may be meaningless.

Suleiman's small life is manageable – even televised interrogations seem distant and Qaddafi's regime and the dissidents' resistance are not always primary concerns for him – but Bahloul represents a world beyond his control that impacts on him directly. Even though he has the capacity to frighten and injure the man, Suleiman is fearful and uncertain about the consequences.

Q Choose an occasion where Bahloul says 'I see you, I see you'. Assuming he is sane, what do you think he might mean?

Sharief

Key quotes

'He had a horrible face, pockmarked like pumice stone.' (p.35)

'His authority was so absolute and sudden it seemed instantly acceptable.' (p.63)

'... I knew that Sharief was still there, loyal ...' (p.142)

Sharief, though a minor character, is important in the story and also has some complexity. We might expect a representative of the Revolutionary Committee to be a clear-cut 'villain', but this is not the case. Matar resists clichés about a character harbouring enmity towards the central characters. Sharief lies and yet he protects. He is responsible for Rashid's disappearance and yet he intervenes in a street fight. He manipulates and yet is gentle with Suleiman.

We first encounter Sharief when Suleiman and Najwa are followed home from town by the Committee car, an incident which is steeped in fear for Suleiman. Later, though, he is strangely drawn to Sharief (p.130) and forms a cautious alliance with him, although he knows Sharief is lying about a friendship with Faraj.

Sharief promises that Najwa and Suleiman's secret about the illicit alcohol is 'safe' with him (p.132): perhaps partly to keep Suleiman on side, or perhaps because he feels a genuine sympathy and compassion for the boy. Later, Sharief intervenes in the fight between Suleiman and the other boys, telling them that they 'can't just hit each other over nothing' (p.164). This is a surprising attitude coming from a man associated with such violence; it forces us to reconsider the possible motivation for what he does, and to see him as a complex, multidimensional character.

Key point

Suleiman says that Sharief is 'loyal to his cause' and admires his 'confidence and youth' (p.156). These are positive traits we might expect to see attributed to the hero or central character in a story, not to one who resembles a villain.

THEMES, IDEAS & VALUES

Innocence

Key quotes

'The innocent ... have no cause to fear; only the guilty live in fear.' (p.8)

'I longed for how things had been.' (p.73)

'Children aren't suppose to know these things.' (p.95)

'I will then be a man, heavy with the world.' (p.142)

'... I couldn't lift her, couldn't carry her, because I was only nine ...' (p.148)

In the Country of Men documents a pivotal summer in a young boy's life, as he inhabits a space somewhere between childhood and adulthood. He seeks the protection of his parents and friends, yet longs for manhood and resents being patronised by adults or his older friends. He is preparing to lose his childhood innocence and the violence and political upheaval of his country speeds up this transition. At the beginning of the summer he occupies himself playing in his garden or with his friends, but by the end of it he is sent abroad for protection from the dangers he has seen befall his neighbours and family.

There are illustrations of the innocence of other characters in the novel, too. For example, Suleiman has an image of his mother 'before the Italian Coffee House' when she was still 'a girl unaware of herself ... sheltered in the clarity of innocence' before she was 'thrust ... over the border and into womanhood, then irrevocably into motherhood' (p.123). This hints at a loss of sexual innocence as well as a loss of the carefree freedom of childhood.

The innocence in *In the Country of Men* refers not just to a blissful, childish state, but also to the innocence of a culture and a country. Sheik Mustafa regularly reminds Suleiman that fear comes from guilt, and that those who are free from guilt are also free from fear. This seems simple, but when we consider the great fear of those who live in opposition to Qaddafi, we are forced to consider, also, our definitions of 'guilt' and 'innocence'. Should Baba fear for his life? Only if he is guilty, according to the religious teaching. But neither Suleiman nor Matar attempt to define guilt, or consider whether the resistance movement is 'wrong'.

Growing up

Although Suleiman watches the televised interrogation alone (and later watches the execution with Mama and Moosa), Baba had previously tried to protect him from having to witness things like this (p.33). Moosa, too, tries to protect him after the Revolutionary Committee men depart: he won't discuss the events with Mama in front of Suleiman (p.69).

While Suleiman appreciates the protection of his parents (especially as relief from his own responsibilities in looking after Mama when Baba is away), he also resists their pampering and repeatedly tells people: 'I am not a child' (p.107 and p.200). When he fights with Kareem in Chapter 9, it is at least partially because the older boys scornfully call him a child. He is sensitive to Kareem's superiority of several years, and desperate to grow up, even though he knows the world is not an easy place for men.

Violence

Violence has the power to destroy innocence. There is a constant threat of violence in the novel; the televised execution and Baba's injuries are graphic illustrations of the dangers facing dissidents in Libya at this time. There is also violence on a smaller and, in some ways, even more disturbing scale. Suleiman's little acts of violence show that his environment is beginning to desensitise him – they are disturbing because he rarely seems to know why he commits them. He sometimes displays remorse, but at other times barely even seems aware of the violence until others try to point out his aggression.

Suleiman's casually violent behaviour suggests that even children are not necessarily innocent of hurting others. Examples include:

- The fight between Suleiman and Kareem; their friend Osama notes that physical fighting is not the way to resolve anything (p.109).
- Suleiman throwing stones at Bahloul as he runs away from the house: when the first stone hits, it makes a 'satisfying thump' and he continues to throw (p.119), but later he notes, 'Something in me was ashamed of what I had done to Bahloul' (p.120).
- Suleiman accidentally hitting Adnan with a stone, which starts a fight with the other boys. Sharief puts a stop to it, saying 'You can't just hit each other over nothing' (p.164).
- Suleiman attempting to drown Bahloul, kicking him in the face (accidentally) and then pushing his head under water (p.218).

Q Are any characters in the novel truly 'innocent'? (Think about the characters' behaviour and how you define 'innocent'.)

Loyalty and betrayal

Key quotes

'Betrayal was a hand squeezing my throat ...' (p.13)

'... what united Kareem and me rarely felt like friendship, but something like blood or virtue.' (p.23)

'How can any one of us prove that he or she is not, and never was, a traitor?' (p.62)

'We drift through allegiances, those we are born into and those we are claimed by, always estranging ourselves.' (p.165)

The notion of loyalty – and its opposite, betrayal – is at the heart of *In the Country of Men*. Nearly every relationship and event in the novel can be discussed in terms of how it illustrates this theme.

Although the text demonstrates that loyalty can cause pain (it can demand great sacrifice and yet still result in loss), the underlying idea is that loyalty must be respected above betrayal. The novel values characters who fight to hold onto the things and people they love and believe in – even if this means making a sacrifice, such as Suleiman's parents make when they send him to Egypt.

Nationalism

The novel is as much a portrait of a country as it is a close study of its central character. Because Libya is a country under political and social strain, characters are defined by their relationship to their country, and by their loyalty and allegiance. When Suleiman settles into life in Cairo he observes that 'Nationalism is as thin as a thread' (p.230), but the evidence in the novel contradicts this. His own loyalty to his country can be measured in the impact that this summer has had on his adult life: though he describes Libya as 'the country that everyone wishes to escape' (p.242), it is still his homeland and he suffers a deep 'emptiness' from its loss, a 'void' Egypt cannot fill (p.233).

Key point

Although they do it for his own protection, and he lies to his mother that it was a good thing to do, Suleiman's exile to Egypt can be seen as one of the deepest betrayals in the novel.

Baba, Rashid, Moosa and Nasser are all motivated in their resistance by a loyalty to the country they have loved before Qaddafi's Revolution, and a passionate belief that they can make a 'better Libya' for their loved ones (p.96). Najwa is unable to share this same nationalism in the face of political and cultural oppression; although she supports her husband, it is because her loyalties are to family more than to country. She tries to do the right thing by Faraj, but says 'I will get my son out of this place if it takes the last of me' (p.97).

Sharief represents all the members of the Mokhabarat: although their loyalty is to Qaddafi and to another version of Libya, it is as valid an example as Baba's. For Suleiman, Sharief is a man who is 'loyal, eternal, sure of his place in the world' (p.180). The binary opposition in *In the Country of Men* is between loyalty and betrayal rather than between 'good' and 'evil'. Although Sharief is a part of the organisation responsible for torture, violence and totalitarian rule, Matar carefully avoids painting him as a 'villain' – rather he is portrayed as someone whose loyalty is to the wrong cause.

Friendship

There are several significant friendships in the novel, each containing betrayals. Najwa and Salma are described as 'two lost sisters who had finally found each other' (p.39). Salma even cares for Najwa on the one occasion when she sees her intoxicated (p.40). But when Rashid is taken, Najwa becomes fearful and withdraws her friendship, demanding that Suleiman do the same with Kareem. Najwa's desire to protect herself and her family comes before loyalty to her neighbour and, in betraying Salma, she loses a friendship.

Faraj and Moosa, too, have a close friendship grounded upon their history and their shared political beliefs. Faraj stood up for Moosa when his father wanted him to pursue a career in law; Moosa 'looked up to him like an older brother' (p.74) and says 'I would give my life for him' (p.95). When Faraj is away, Moosa cares for his friend's family (and later provides refuge for Suleiman in Egypt), and it is Moosa who fetches Faraj when he is released from his incarceration.

When Faraj is finally home, though, Moosa seems to suffer a kind of displaced survivor guilt: Faraj is alive because Mama intervened and asked for Ustath Jafer's help. Moosa sees this as a betrayal when others have died for the cause and he is unable to see progress with the resistance. Moosa 'can't bear looking at him ... The betrayal in his eyes' (p.207) and, shortly afterwards, he accepts his deportation back to Egypt. Once in Egypt, as far as we know, he – like Suleiman – does not see Faraj again.

Suleiman and Kareem's friendship echoes Najwa and Salma's, though with a childish unawareness. Najwa's fear is tangible and she is able to articulate her withdrawal from Salma (p.40). But Suleiman's betrayal of his and Kareem's loyalty to each other is less explicable. After Rashid is taken he finds himself unable to spend time with Kareem, whom he has previously considered a blood brother. In Chapter 9 we see the sadness this has caused them both, though neither is able to articulate or repair the situation (pp.105–10), and when there is a moment where they might reconcile it instead escalates into an argument. They never recover from this, even when, many years later, Kareem attempts to reach out to Suleiman. Though he longs for their childhood friendship (p.237), Kareem represents a past that Suleiman cannot forgive and, to make matters worse, is now engaged to Siham whom Suleiman had loved.

This is not the first instance of Suleiman betraying a friend. He recalls an incident when he skipped school with another boy and, when punished, lied that it was the other boy's idea (pp.153–4). Although he claims it 'didn't feel wrong at the time', when he saw how his lie affected the other boy he recognised his betrayal and felt terrible. The experience stayed with him and he recalls it when he feels 'sick' and 'dizzy' (p.153) on realising that he has betrayed Nasser to the stranger who tapped their phone conversation (p.141).

There is one friendship in the novel that illustrates an ultimate loyalty, or 'the opposite of betrayal' (p.116): that of Rashid towards Faraj. The book Suleiman rescues from Najwa and Moosa's burning happens to be one given to Faraj by Rashid. It is inscribed 'To my eternal friend and comrade ... With my undying loyalty' (p.105), and Rashid keeps his word. When he is publicly interrogated before his execution, Rashid lies to protect Faraj, perhaps saving Faraj's life even when he cannot save his own.

Q How does the novel condemn betrayal?

Q How would you define loyalty?

Heroism

Key quotes

'... I often lay in my darkened bedroom dreaming of saving her.' (p.12)

'Here it's either silence or exile, walk by the wall or leave. Go be a hero elsewhere.' (p.53)

'You can't give people braver hearts.' (p.55)

'It's one thing not to fear death, another to sing under its sword.' (p.67)

The image of the 'hero' is a recurring motif in *In the Country of Men*. It is often associated with surviving violence, but also with saving others. The novel endorses the idea that heroes can offer us courage and something to aspire to – Suleiman, for example, looks up to his hero Scheherazade and finds inspiration in her strength. At the same time, Matar warns that heroism is a fantasy that cannot be upheld, and that we will always be let down by our heroes.

Many kinds of hero are portrayed in the novel, from Adnan, who lives life bravely under the threat of his disease (pp.127–8); to the fictional Scheherazade; to Faraj, who is a hero of sorts to his son and a hero to Moosa (pp.95–8).

Rescue fantasies

Suleiman has a recurring fantasy of rescuing his mother – particularly in the past, when she was a child, so as to prevent her later suffering. Mama may have contributed to these fantasies, often describing her son as her 'beautiful prince' (p.82) and casting him in a classical fairytale role: 'You are my prince. One day you'll be a man and take me away on your white horse' (p.12).

Since Suleiman has grown up with this expectation, it is hardly surprising that he fantasises about being able to rescue his young mother. For example, when Mama tells stories about her unhappy arranged marriage, Suleiman in his imagination is able to prevent it: '... I could have saved her then, when she was fourteen, before what happened happened ... running away somewhere ... where no one could ever find us' (p.148).

Cinematic and historical heroes

A recurring image, evoked by movies Suleiman has seen, is of wounded men who are heroes by virtue of their survival. Their trials are usually evidenced by wounds and blood, and Suleiman is clear that everyone respects 'a bleeding man' (p.36). It is easy for him to respect someone whose challenges have been physical and have left visable evidence. He imagines Baba returning home, 'leaning with one arm against the door, sweating, bleeding beautifully from one eyebrow and panting – exactly like the heroes I saw in films' (p.61).

This fantasy is followed by a similar image of his mother after the Committee men leave: he hears the fear in her voice 'like during the final moments when the heroine, holding on for dear life, attempts to deliver her last words' (p.65). The extension of the image in this particular instance is that Suleiman wishes he could be the person to receive those desperate last words and offer her comfort.

After Rashid's public interrogation, Suleiman imagines him 'handcuffed on the floor, cheeks crimson, a heroic drip of blood from one corner of his mouth' (p.121), and compares the lie to protect Faraj with the heroism of the black American slaves he once saw in a documentary. When they stood up together against their white masters, Suleiman saw his father 'poised in admiration' for the slaves as they downed their tools and clapped in unison (p.121). For Suleiman, heroism is characterised by drama and spectacle, just as it is in films he has seen.

Interestingly, when Baba at last returns home, wounded, Suleiman is confronted by reality and his injured father does not inspire his admiration in the way that the injured heroes in films had. Reality is a frightening disappointment compared to the cinema.

Scheherazade

Scheherazade, a fictional character who keeps herself alive by telling a thousand and one wonderful stories to her captor, the king, is Suleiman's hero. He learns of her through his mother, whose own mother memorised the entire story and would recite it to her children (pp.15–16). Mama herself is scornful of the story, saying Suleiman should find another hero because Scheherazade 'accepted slavery over death' (p.15). For Mama this is not admirable, but for Suleiman, Scheherazade 'was one of the bravest people that had ever lived. It's one thing not to fear death, another to sing under its sword' (p.67).

When Suleiman himself needs 'bravery' the first time he speaks with Sharief, he thinks of Scheherazade and although she inspires him, his feelings are coloured by his mother's scorn; even his hero cannot help him (p.129).

Q Why do you think Suleiman admires Scheherazade? (Find evidence in the text to support your answer.)

Q How does the novel show us that heroes cannot live up to our expectations?

Morality and religion

Key quotes

'It's our obligation to call injustice by its name.' (p.53)

'... God never forgets the faithful.' (p.53)

'Whenever someone is very upset or angry, ask them to praise the Prophet and they have to stop yelling or crying and praise.' (p.81)

Islam is a strong and ubiquitous (present everywhere) part of Suleiman and his family's life so that when he seeks explanation for the world around him, he regularly turns to religion. Sometimes this is playful and childlike, as with the mulberries he eats in Chapter 4: he constructs a story about the angels bringing mulberries to earth, to ease human lives with their deliciousness. This imaginative explanation follows facts and rules that he knows from his religious study – for example, he recalls that God is 'Allknowing', so of course saw what the angels were doing, but decided to permit it (p.48).

The playful scenario Suleiman constructs is a way of reinforcing his religious education as well as simply passing the time. A similar episode occurs when he plays barefoot on his roof in the heat and is reminded of the story of the 'Bridge to Paradise' and how hot the flames from Hell will be. For him, the religious story is as real as his own material daily life and he integrates one into the other, barely differentiating between the concrete and the philosophical/theological constructs (pp.45–6).

A similar integration occurs the first time he witnesses his parents having sex. He is not equipped emotionally to deal with the physical or psychological implications of what he has seen (for example, he does not fully understand his mother's unhappiness) but instead considers the event in terms of his religious knowledge, wondering if 'God's Seat' was disturbed in the same way as his own heart (p.88). Though his interpretation is not completely accurate, a religious explanation of the bodily world is the first one to come to mind for him. He even wonders if 'Providence' sent him, intending him to rescue his mother (see the discussion on his rescue fantasies in 'Heroism' for more on this), and judges himself for failing in the task (p.88).

Religion for Suleiman is not just a set of stories but an instruction in living and, as with other elements of his life, he is at an age where he is beginning to have an awareness of these processes. When he eats the mulberries, for example, he questions whether he is stealing them and, if so, whether he will be forgiven. He doesn't explicitly consider the religious principles he may be breaking, but only a page earlier he had discussed God's forgiveness for the angels' mischief in permitting Adam and Eve the mulberries in their earthly exile. This incident demonstrates how important religious strictures are in Suleiman's everyday life, and how they contribute to his nascent sense of morality.

Parents and children

Key quotes

'Mama was ill again ... where is Baba? He should be here because when he's home everything is normal, she is never ill, and I am never woken up like this to find everything changed.' (p.10)

'I imagined how it might be to live without her ... I wasn't sure if it was fear or excitement that I felt at the thought of losing her.' (p.17)

'Mama and I spent most of the time together – she alone, I unable to leave her.' (p.21)

'The times I felt closest to him were when he was unaware of my presence ...' (p.29)

'Can you become a man without becoming your father?' (p.149)

Family and children are shown to be very important in Libyan social and religious culture. Suleiman explains this in Chapter 3, when he considers the fact that:

> parents with only one offspring were always at the risk of leading people to believe that either the woman was no longer good, or, God forbid, both the mother and the father were objecting to God's Will. (p.23)

Children, Suleiman has heard people say, 'reinvent life and make black days rosy' (pp.241–2). The implicit view embodied in the text is that children are to be desired and valued. In return, Suleiman loves his parents deeply and when they send him to Egypt, although it is for his own protection, he is devastated by the separation:

> I looked back and saw Mama in Baba's arms. There they were, the two people I loved the most ... huddled together in the empty airport, disappearing. Is this the time to wave? But I could no longer see them. In every direction I turned they weren't there. (p.227)

One of the central themes in the novel is of Suleiman navigating his relationship with his family. He is poised to enter a new, more adult phase of life, and part of this is attaining an understanding of how he fits into his own family.

Mother and son

Suleiman has a close but ambivalent relationship with his mother, and one that is growing more complex as he grows older. In the first chapter he is upset by her 'illness', yet he is still captivated by 'her beautiful face' (p.1) and wants to 'run to her, to hold her hand, latch on to her dress as she shopped and dealt with the world, a world full of men and the greed of men' (p.3). In the middle of the book he describes a particular indulgence and joy, that of slipping in beside his mother as she sleeps on the couch to cuddle with her on early winter mornings before he goes to school:

> when the sky remained stubbornly dark, I sneaked into her makeshift bed fully dressed ... I coiled within the cave of her blanket, my cheek warmed by her pillow, wondering how can Heaven be anything other than this? (p.86)

The affection continues, and in the final chapter, although he is anxious about seeing her again after so long, he cries out excitedly when she appears. The final words in the novel describe their greeting as she kisses him, combs his hair with her fingers and straightens his collar – gentle affectionate touches that he is ready to accept (pp.244–5).

Suleiman, then, has a deep and enduring love for his mother. Indeed, he identifies her as the root of all love, and yet it is far from a simple love: 'There was anger, there was pity, even the dark warm embrace of hate, but always love and always the joy that surrounds the beginning of love' (p.21). This represents a common experience of relationships between children and parents, especially at an age where children are preparing to embrace adulthood and relinquish some of the habits and comforts of childhood. There is a desire to resist parental influence and simultaneously a need for the security and support that parents can offer.

Suleiman's relationship with his mother is also complicated by the fact that he is an only child and she often turns to him, solely, for support when Baba is away. During these times she drinks heavily and expects Suleiman to care for her and to listen to her obsessive and secretive retellings of the 'black day' (p.11, p.144, p.146) of her marriage to Faraj. He resents being burdened with these responsibilities, both emotional and practical. He even occasionally imagines life without her, suspecting he might be better off. Yet, at the height of the crisis when Baba is missing, it is exactly this ritual that he craves as comfort: for the first time, he begs her to tell him her old stories (pp.167–8).

Key point

Despite the complexities of their relationship, Suleiman is still simply a child who loves his mother deeply. Even when he goes on a day trip to Lepcis, he is reluctant to leave her: 'I felt a string in my heart break as I looked back at Mama waving goodbye' (p.25).

Father and son

The relationship between Suleiman and Baba is secondary to the mother–son relationship in the novel, though it echoes the conflicts and ambivalence. Baba is kind and loving to Suleiman, but also distant, withdrawn and absent – often literally, when he is away on business, or after the Committee takes him.

When Baba is away, Suleiman misses him because of the extra strain it places on him in caring for his mother (she is never 'ill' when Baba is home) and his homecoming is to be celebrated: 'I felt such relief now that Baba was home' (p.44). Baba is there not only to protect Mama, but also to make the house a safe place for all of them. Suleiman also misses his father because he has a genuine affection for him. Before Baba was taken, when his father went away on business trips Suleiman wanted desperately to go with him: 'I begged him several times and once I felt so sick with sadness that I screamed, kicked his shins and pummelled his thighs' (p.29).

After Baba returns from his ordeal with the Revolutionary Committee, Suleiman wonders what life might be like without not just Mama but Baba too – he again feels 'a flutter of excitement' in his stomach, and has shameful fantasies of 'losing those' he 'loved the most' (p.198). This is perhaps simply a part of his growing up and negotiating his relationship with his parents. When Suleiman does leave his parents, at the airport, it is not by choice and he feels keenly a loss of security and love rather than an excitement at gaining independence.

Q How does the novel convey the love between Suleiman and Baba?

DIFFERENT INTERPRETATIONS

Different interpretations arise from different responses to a text. Over time, a text will give rise to a wide range of responses from its readers, who may come from various social or cultural groups and live in very different places and historical periods. These responses can be published in newspapers, journals and books by critics and reviewers, or they can be expressed in discussions among readers in the media, classrooms, book groups and so on. While there is no single correct reading or interpretation of a text, it is important to understand that an interpretation is more than a personal opinion – it is the justification of a point of view on the text. To present an interpretation of the text based on your point of view you must use a logical argument and support it with relevant evidence from the text.

The critics' viewpoints

While responses to any work will always vary, a work like this, one that is both recent and multi-award-winning, tends to have consistently positive responses. However, the focus of each review will indicate its differing interpretation.

Kamila Shamsie, for example, in her review in the *Guardian* concentrates on both religious and political themes, as well as the relationships between the characters (Shamsie 2006). Lorraine Adams' *New York Times* review identifies as a central theme 'the convoluted roots of betrayal'; she concentrates her reading more on Suleiman's personal story than on either the family relationships or the broader political setting (Adams 2007). She also links these issues to the events in Matar's own life. David Dabydeen, in his review in the *Independent*, is most interested in the political events in the novel, and how the politics under a dictatorship are echoed in the domestic politics.

Two out of three of these reviews, however, specifically highlight the poetic style of Matar's prose, each choosing certain moments to cite. So while readers will find different themes and ideas within a text, they will also often share a common experience of the text.

Two possible interpretations

The following examples demonstrate how observations about the same facts can be used to support two very different interpretations of a text, as long as the evaluation is supported with textual evidence.

Reading 1

***In the Country of Men* demonstrates that political resistance is naive and futile.**

Although the focus of *In the Country of Men* is Suleiman's domestic existence, the narrative also tells a story of a country under a frightening dictatorship and in political turmoil. Many of the central characters (particularly Faraj, Rashid, Moosa and Nasser) are involved in an underground resistance movement, fighting optimistically for a 'better Libya' (p.96). We only see this from Suleiman's perspective, so we lack detailed information about their goals, activities and practices. But we do see their attempts to inspire and mobilise others through the leaflet campaign (pp.33–4) and we know they meet secretly in Faraj's house and at the Martyrs' Square headquarters.

However, the outcomes of resistance in the novel are only negative. Qaddafi's Mokhabarat conducts public interrogations of 'traitors' (those, like Rashid and Faraj, who do not support his regime) and its presence is everywhere. Phone lines are often tapped and the men of the Revolutionary Committee, like Sharief, are powerful and frightening. They maintain surveillance on anyone suspected of being a traitor and take people away from their homes and families to incarcerate, interrogate, torture or even execute them.

Rashid provides an example of how futile resistance is: he is interrogated and eventually publicly executed for his beliefs and activities. His neighbours withdraw their friendship and support from his family, who eventually escape to another city for their safety. Despite Rashid lying to protect him, Faraj too is arrested and interrogated. However, Baba is at least returned home alive, through his wife's intervention when she effectively aligns herself with the Mokhabarat. Najwa – who does not support the resistance – welcomes her husband home and there is no indication that he will rejoin the resistance movement even when he heals. Moosa, their friend, is disillusioned by the futility of the underground movement's experiences and does not object when he is deported back to Egypt; he has seemingly given up hope for his adopted homeland of Libya.

The novel does not show any positive outcomes of the resistance. Suleiman is sent to Egypt for his own protection and watches from afar as the social, political and financial struggles continue for those left behind in Libya. Faraj is arrested for a seemingly innocent activity after many years of being dissociated from the resistance. His past involvement is enough to mark him as a traitor; he dies not long after being released in an amnesty.

The resistance movement in *In the Country of Men* is rewarded only by death, loss and grief: the novel offers no hope that resistance can enact political change or improve lives.

Reading 2

***In the Country of Men* argues that political resistance is a vital part of a healthy community and is to be celebrated.**

Although the Libyan resistance movement is rarely rewarded in *In the Country of Men* and its proponents suffer pain, loss, grief and even death, Matar's novel celebrates those who give their lives for their political beliefs.

The novel's most admirable characters are Rashid and Moosa. They are respected by others and in their behaviour we understand why. Rashid is educated, kind, loving towards his family, loyal to his friends and, above all, so dedicated to his political cause that he dies for it. While the novel does not celebrate his death, it celebrates his life, presenting him as a role model for young Libyans like his students, his son and his son's friends. By making Rashid a loyal resistance fighter as well as a likeable and laudable character, Matar suggests that we should respect and celebrate those who are prepared to die for a cause.

Moosa, similarly, is one of the more likeable characters in the novel – compassionate, intelligent, affectionate and loyal – and he, too, is (mostly) dedicated to the cause. Faraj is also a respected character and Suleiman's admiration and affection for Rashid, Moosa and Faraj strongly guides the reader's view of them. By associating the admirable characters with the resistance, the novel shows us how 'good' people fight for what they believe in – we are encouraged to empathise with them, understand their challenges and hope for their success.

The novel shows that, without the resistance, the country would live without hope, in constant fear and unhappiness. Najwa, who opposes the resistance movement because she sees it as futile and dangerous, illustrates this well. For her own and her family's safety, she would rather they all stay under the radar and avoid drawing attention to themselves; she is prepared to sacrifice both the country they love and also the basic human right of freedom.

QUESTIONS & ANSWERS

This section focuses on your own analytical writing on the text, and gives you strategies for producing high quality responses in your coursework and exam essays.

Essay writing – an overview

An essay on a literary text is a formal and serious piece of writing that presents your point of view on the text, usually in response to a given essay topic. Your 'point of view' in an essay is your interpretation of the meaning of the text's language, structure, characters, situations and events, supported by detailed analysis of textual evidence.

Analyse – don't summarise

In your essays it is important to avoid simply summarising what happens in a text.

- A **summary** is a description or paraphrase (retelling in different words) of the characters and events. For example: 'Macbeth has a horrifying vision of a dagger dripping with blood before he goes to murder King Duncan.'
- An **analysis** is an explanation of the real meaning or significance that lies 'beneath' the text's words (and images, for a film). For example: 'Macbeth's vision of a bloody dagger shows how deeply uneasy he is about the violent act he is contemplating – as well as his sense that supernatural forces are impelling him to act.'

A limited amount of summary is sometimes necessary to let your reader know which part of the text you wish to discuss. However, always keep this to a minimum and follow it immediately with your analysis (explanation) of what this part of the text is really telling us.

Plan your essay

Carefully plan your essay so that you have a clear idea of what you are going to say. The plan ensures that your ideas flow logically, that your argument remains consistent and that you stay on the topic. An essay plan should be a list of **brief dot points** – no more than half a page.

- Include your central argument or main contention – a concise statement (usually in a single sentence) of your overall response to the topic. See 'Analysing a sample topic' for guidelines on how to formulate a main contention.
- Write three or four dot points for each paragraph indicating the main idea and evidence/examples from the text. Note that in your essay you will need to *expand* on these points and *analyse* the evidence.

Structure your essay

An essay is a complete, self-contained piece of writing. It has a clear beginning (the introduction), middle (several body paragraphs) and end (the last paragraph or conclusion). It must also have a central argument that runs throughout, linking each paragraph to form a coherent whole.

See examples of introductions and conclusions in the 'Analysing a sample topic' and 'Sample answer' sections.

The introduction establishes your overall response to the topic. It includes your main contention and outlines the main evidence you will refer to in the course of the essay. Write your introduction *after* you have done a plan and *before* you write the rest of the essay.

The body paragraphs argue your case – they present evidence from the text and explain how this evidence supports your argument. Each body paragraph needs:

- a strong **topic sentence** (usually the first sentence) that states the main point being made in the paragraph
- **evidence** from the text, including some brief quotations
- **analysis** of the textual evidence explaining its significance and **explanation** of how it supports your argument
- **links back to the topic** in one or more statements, usually towards the end of the paragraph.

Connect the body paragraphs so that your discussion flows smoothly. Use some linking words and phrases like 'similarly' and 'on the other hand', though don't start every paragraph like this. Another strategy is to use a significant word from the last sentence of one paragraph in the first sentence of the next.

Use key terms from the topic – or synonyms for them – throughout, so the relevance of your discussion to the topic is always clear.

The conclusion ties everything together and finishes the essay. It includes strong statements that emphasise your central argument and provide a clear response to the topic.

Avoid simply restating the points made earlier in the essay – this will end on a very flat note and imply that you have run out of ideas and vocabulary. The conclusion is meant to be a logical extension of what you have written, not just a repetition or summary of it. Writing an effective conclusion can be a challenge. Try using these tips:

- Start by linking back to the final sentence of the second-last paragraph – this helps your writing to 'flow', rather than just leaping back to your main contention straight away.
- Use synonyms and expressions with equivalent meanings to vary your vocabulary. This allows you to reinforce your line of argument without being repetitive.
- When planning your essay, think of one or two broad statements or observations about the text's wider meaning. These should be related to the topic and your overall argument. Keep them for the conclusion, since they will give you something 'new' to say but still follow logically from your discussion. The introduction will be focused on the topic, but the conclusion can present a wider view of the text.

Essay topics

1 'Although the narrator is only a nine-year-old boy, his voice is that of a much older person.' How does Matar achieve this, and to what purpose?

2 'Sharief and Rashid are two very different people.' Discuss.

3 Is *In the Country of Men* a domestic or a political story?

4 'Suleiman is a boy poised to enter "the country of men".' Discuss.

5 When Rashid is taken, Suleiman says the Revolutionary Committee car is "like a giant dead moth in the sun". How does Matar employ symbolism in the novel?

6 'Najwa is the central character in *In the Country of Men*.' Discuss.

7 Rashid lies during his interrogation in order to protect Faraj, and Suleiman calls this "the opposite of betrayal". What does the novel argue about the importance of loyalty?

8 Hisham Matar has said that "Children live with an intensity most adults take for granted." How does *In the Country of Men* illustrate this idea?

9 'Libya is merely an incidental backdrop for Suleiman's story.' Discuss.

10 "Egypt has not replaced Libya." How does the summer of 1979 shape Suleiman's feelings about his homeland?

Vocabulary for writing on *In the Country of Men*

Autobiographical elements: The novel is a work of fiction and should not be confused with autobiography (nonfiction). However it does contain a number of autobiographical elements (such as the fact that Matar, like Suleiman, grew up in Libya), which you may want to discuss when analysing the work.

Dissident: Although the word is not used in the novel (instead 'traitor' is usually adopted), this would be an appropriate term for any member of the resistance movement. The word describes an individual who disagrees with or won't comply with the dominant political system in place.

Islam: The religion adhered to by those of Muslim faith. The ***Quran*** is the principal sacred text of Islam and documents the word of the Prophet, Mohammed.

Totalitarian: Although, again, the word is not used in the novel, Libya under Qaddafi can be described as a totalitarian regime: political and social governance that does not permit differing views and belief systems.

Unreliable narrator: This is a literary term describing a narrator whose knowledge, opinions and/or voice differ in some way from the authorial voice. In Suleiman's case, his age makes him unreliable because his knowledge and understanding are limited, and we are often able to read more into what he says than he is aware of.

(Also see the Glossary at the end of this text guide.)

Analysing a sample topic

'Although the narrator is only a nine-year-old boy, his voice is that of a much older person.' How does Matar achieve this, and to what purpose?

This is a complex essay topic beginning with a comment on the text and concluding with a question about the construction of the text. Start by identifying key words or phrases:

- narrator
- voice
- how does Matar achieve
- purpose.

Be sure you understand what these mean; the first two, in this case, are technical terms, and the second two refer to form and technique, and impact and meaning.

Paraphrase into your own words what the question is asking of you: in this case, something like 'how does the author blend a youthful character with a mature character and how does this affect the reader?' Next, form a main contention or argument (a kind of 'answer' to the essay question). For example, 'Matar uses sophisticated imagery to accompany the child's tale, so that his work is both emotional and complex.' A question like this does not ask you to agree or disagree, but to express an opinion supported by evidence from the text.

Sample introduction

> The central character in *In the Country of Men*, Suleiman, is a child. We know this from Matar's language choices (such as the structure of Suleiman's sentences) as well as from the experiences he undergoes during the novel. Yet at the same time, we are aware that the narrative is being filtered through the voice of an older Suleiman. This dual perspective allows Matar to harness both the innocent idiosyncrasies of childhood, and also the articulate, compelling authority of adulthood.

Body paragraph outline

Paragraph 1 – describe which elements of the text inform us that the narrator is a child:

- Note facts that Suleiman does not fully understand, such as that his mother's 'illness' is actually drunkenness; these suggest childlike innocence.
- Consider technical aspects such as the length of Suleiman's sentences and the complexity of his vocabulary.
- Identify examples of childish behaviour, such as when Suleiman has a tantrum because Baba won't let him come abroad (p.29).
- Describe Suleiman's relationship with his mother, referring to specific moments when we are aware of his youth, such as Suleiman's reluctance to leave her to visit Lepcis (p.22–5).

Paragraph 2 – identify the techniques Matar uses to integrate an 'adult' awareness into Suleiman's story:

- Note occasions when the voice of the 'adult' Suleiman intrudes into the text, explaining how his childhood affects his adult life, e.g. 'Later, when I discovered ... Judge Yaseen was to become my guardian' (p.74).
- Identify sophisticated uses of language, such as the analogy of his mother as a film heroine, which employs complex, formal syntax and a highly developed vocabulary, e.g. 'an infinite intimacy is born, a trust unbound and unhindered by the possibility of betrayal' (p.66).
- Identify uses of language that create strong imagery, such as 'I felt a string in my heart break' (p.25) – which is a mature image to describe a childish emotion.

Paragraph 3 – discuss how the combination of the younger and older voice impacts on the reader:

- Explain how the 'adult' perspective has a practical purpose, allowing Matar to give readers information beyond his central character's knowledge.

- Develop the idea that the youthful innocence juxtaposed beside the resigned nostalgia increases the emotional impact of the novel, allowing us multiple perspectives on the story.
- Illustrate how the integration of two convincing versions of one character's voice adds depth and complexity to the novel.

Sample conclusion

> *In the Country of Men* tells the story of a young boy in the process of becoming a man against a backdrop of a country in political turmoil. With careful modulation of language, Matar creates two distinct narrative voices; the inclusion of both a childlike and an adult voice enables Matar to reach his audience through multiple channels, strengthening the work's impact. The childish innocence contrasts with the harsh, violent reality of Libya under Qaddafi, and Suleiman's adult perspective contextualises his childhood experience.

SAMPLE ANSWER

'Sharief and Rashid are two very different people.' Discuss.

Sharief and Rashid are men from opposite sides of the Libyan political conflict in the 1970s, but they are more similar than might at first be expected. While we are inclined to simply judge one as a hero and one as a villain, this would ignore the similarities in their characters, simplify the themes of the novel and diminish the richness and complexity in Matar's writing.

We know that Rashid is a 'good' person. He is educated and informed, and respected by his students at the university, with whom he is familiar and for whom he demonstrates pastoral care. For example, he jokes with them when he takes them to Lepcis and when two of them fight with each other, he gently puts a stop to the fight, physically risking his own well-being by deciding to 'put himself between them'. He is also affectionate towards and loved by his son – Suleiman admires their closeness and sometimes wishes his own father were more like Rashid. Finally, Rashid is loyal to his political cause and also shows 'undying loyalty' to his friends; when interrogated as a traitor, he lies to protect his friend Faraj. He is eventually executed for his loyalty to his cause (resistance against the Qaddafi regime). He is not violent and, even when he is seized by the Committee, 'didn't struggle'. But is he really a hero?

Despite his many admirable qualities, Rashid still has flaws. It could be argued, for example, that Rashid's dedication to his cause was foolish and selfish: when he is executed he leaves behind a wife and son who must fend for themselves in a strongly patriarchal society. Perhaps he should have prioritised the wellbeing of his family over the philosophical idealism of a political belief? Also, we know that Rashid lies when interrogated; he denies Faraj's involvement in the resistance. Certainly, this could be seen to be heroic, since it is in the interest of saving his friend. But viewed from a strict moral or religious perspective, lying should never be respected or excused; and in this case Rashid only lies to protect his friend, while betraying other members of the resistance. So Rashid is not completely blameless; rather he is a passionate man who will go to great lengths to fight for what he believes in.

Sharief could be described in exactly the same way. Although we do not know what motivates him to join the Revolutionary Committee, we do see that he is 'loyal to his cause'. He does his job with determination and commitment, never wavering from his task. Like Rashid, he believes that his politics are worthy of his commitment and he even believes that they are worthy of others' lives.

Like Rashid, Sharief is prepared to lie in the interests of furthering his cause. He tells Suleiman he is a friend of Faraj, hoping Suleiman will give him information about his father and other dissidents. He manipulates Suleiman, and his lying makes him untrustworthy. We know that he was one of the men who took Rashid and that he did so with violence – a trait we are not encouraged to respect. But is he a villain?

There is a key incident in the novel that prevents us from seeing Sharief as simply a 'bad guy'. This is when he intervenes in the boys' fight in the street. He steps in to stop a physical fight – in much the same way that Rashid did with his students – and says to the boys: 'You can't just hit each other over nothing'. This echoes the pastoral role Rashid plays with his students; in both cases the men are preventing violence and attempting to educate younger people in moral behaviour.

These personality traits and events show us how alike Sharief and Rashid are. They are both zealous men who are loyal to their causes – to the extent that they are prepared to lie for them. Neither will tolerate violence that they see as unnecessary and will step into physical fights to prevent such violence. The main difference between the men is where their political loyalties lie.

One of the strengths of Matar's writing is his ability to create, in even a short novel, complex characters with depth rather than clichéd or simplistic heroes and villains. He paints a portrait of a time and place where violence is part of the culture – both politically and personally – and while the novel doesn't condemn violence, nor does it celebrate it. Similarly, he never allows us to see his characters as clearly 'good' or 'evil'. Instead, they are nuanced and realistic and behave according to their own morals and beliefs in whatever situation they find themselves. Sharief and Rashid are two examples of such characters, and they differ only in circumstance.

REFERENCES & READING

Text

Matar, Hisham 2012, *In the Country of Men*, Penguin, London. First published 2006.

Newspaper articles

Adams, Lorraine 2007, 'The Dissident's Son', *New York Times*, 4 March, www.nytimes.com/2007/03/04/books/review/Adams.t.html

Dabydeen, David 2006, '*In the Country of Men* by Hisham Matar: Love in Libya's time of tyranny', *Independent*, 14 July, www.independent.co.uk/arts-entertainment/books/reviews/in-the-country-of-men-by-hisham-matar-407808.html

Matar, Hisham 2010, *Untitled*, 16 January, www.guardian.co.uk/books/2010/jan/16/hisham-matar-father-libyan-jail

Shamsie, Kamila 2006, 'Where the Mulberries Grow', *Guardian*, 29 July, www.guardian.co.uk/books/2006/jul/29/featuresreviews.guardianreview19

Websites

Gilbert, Harriet and Matar, Hisham 2011, *Interview*, 3 September, www.bbc.co.uk/iplayer/episode/p00jszv2/World_Book_Club_Hisham_Matar_In_The_Country_Of_Men/

majjal.wordpress.com/2011/10/31/lecture-hisham-matar-in-the-country-of-men-oct-7-2011/

This site houses a video of a lecture by given in 2011 by Matar at a US college; the middle section discusses this novel.

Matar, Hisham no date, *About the Author*, http://www.randomhouse.com/book/109006/in-the-country-of-men-by-hisham-matar#authorq&a

Musiitwa, Daniel 2011, *Award Winning Author Hisham Matar on the 2011 Caine Prize*, http://www.africabookclub.com/?p=3965

Tarbush, Susannah 2006, *In the Country of Men,* http://www.libyaforum.org/archive/index.php?option=com_content&task=view&id=3322&Itemid=239

Other references

Cuddon, J. A. 1988, *Dictionary of Literary Terms and Literary Theory,* Penguin, London.

Vandewalle, Dirk 2006, *A History of Modern Libya,* Cambridge University Press, Cambridge.

GLOSSARY

Afandi: term of respect for a learned and successful man.

Antenna: informal description used for members of the Revolutionary Committee or the Mokhabarat.

Eid: traditional religious holiday or festival observed in the Islamic faith. It celebrates sacrifice to God (as in Abraham's sacrifice), usually occurring in late October (but varies based on the Islamic calendar).

Habibi: affectionate nickname or term bestowed upon males (for females, the word differs slightly).

Hajj: religious pilgrimage every Muslim is expected to carry out at least once in their life. It is performed by hundreds of thousands of people each year; it includes the journey to Mecca and the performance of numerous symbolic rituals, sacrifices and celebrations.

Haram: has a number of meanings; the one used here is for something forbidden according to religious law (as in Mama's 'medicine').

Jallabia: traditional item of clothing; similar to a kaftan and worn by both men and women.

Mokhabarat: the organisation of those who support and enforce Qaddafi's rule.

Quran: central religious text in the Islamic faith; believed to contain the word of God.

Sunna: accompaniment to the Quran; offers further instruction on the ways to practice religious observance.

Surah: section of the Quran.